MW01108480

Access To
High Hope

Second Lesson Sermons
For Lent/Easter

Cycle A

Harry N. Huxhold

CSS Publishing Company, Inc., Lima, Ohio

ACCESS TO HIGH HOPE

Library of Congress Cataloging-in-Publication Data

Huxhold, Harry N.
    Access to high hope : second lesson sermons for Lent/Easter, cycle A / Harry N.
Huxhold.
        p. cm.
    ISBN 0-7880-1828-0 (alk. paper)
    1. Lenten sermons. 2. Holy-Week sermons. 3. Easter—Sermons. 4. Eastertide—Ser-
mons. 5. Bible. N.T. Epistles—Sermons. 6. Sermons, American—20th century. I. Title.
BV4277 .H89 2001
252'.62—dc21
                                                              2001025104
                                                                      CIP

For more information about CSS Publishing Company resources, visit our website at
www.csspub.com.

ISBN 0-7880-1828-0   PRINTED IN U.S.A.

In memory

of

our son

Timothy Joel

who achieved the high hope

in our Lord Jesus Christ

Table Of Contents

Introduction 7

Ash Wednesday 9
Lent Is About Reconciliation
2 Corinthians 5:20b—6:10

Lent 1 17
The Beginning Of It All
Romans 5:12-19

Lent 2 25
Abraham, Our Father
Romans 4:1-5, 13-17

Lent 3 33
Access To Grace
Romans 5:1-11

Lent 4 41
Live In The Light
Ephesians 5:8-14

Lent 5 49
A Higher Lifestyle
Romans 8:6-11

Passion/Palm Sunday 57
A Meeting Of The Minds
Philippians 2:5-11

Maundy Thursday 65
All Baked Into One Loaf
1 Corinthians 11:23-26

Good Friday   **73**
The New And Living Way
Hebrews 10:16-25

Easter   **81**
Easter Is About You
Colossians 3:1-4

Easter 2   **89**
The Outcome Of Faith
1 Peter 1:3-9

Easter 3   **97**
Genuine Mutual Love
1 Peter 1:17-23

Easter 4   **105**
Credit For Suffering
1 Peter 2:19-25

Easter 5   **113**
Identity As A People
1 Peter 2:2-10

Easter 6   **121**
The Blessing In Suffering
1 Peter 3:13-22

Ascension Of The Lord   **129**
Having High Hope
Ephesians 1:15-23

Easter 7   **137**
Surprised By Suffering?
1 Peter 4:12-14; 5:6-11

Introduction

The lessons for Lent and Easter in *The Revised Common Lectionary* are just what they say "for Lent and Easter." The former lectionaries were shaped by the tradition that the Sundays in Lent were not of Lent. The presumption was that the meditations and devotions on the passion and death of our Lord Jesus Christ would be observed on the weekdays of the Lenten period of forty fasting days. The change from the Sundays in Lent to the current Sundays of Lent is no more obvious than on the Passion Sunday, formerly Palm Sunday. Palm Sunday traditionally was a day of high celebration. In transition Palm Sunday now becomes the day of our Lord's Passion when we rehearse the entire account of our Lord's Passion.

The innovation of lessons for Lenten Sundays more pointed to the consideration of the significance of our Lord's passion are indeed welcome. Regrettably we recognize that the past observances of weekday Lenten devotion and preaching are long gone. The sociology of the modern family is not conducive nor supportive of the Lenten programs of services and preaching. The liturgiologists recognized the economy of worship time families practice and have wisely surrendered the Sundays in Lent to be of Lent.

The second readings, or epistles, are especially helpful in expressing and explaining the meaning of our Lord's passion and resurrection. The disciples of our Lord, who witnessed the passion and resurrection of our Lord, had no perception of what those experiences meant until they examined the Hebrew Scriptures to find their meaning. The apostolic epistles do that for us. The epistles bring the events of our Lord's life together with their interpretation in the light of what God had been revealing all along that we might find the significance of the Christ events in our lives.

Another improvement in the revised lectionary program is the change from naming the Sundays after Easter to be the Sundays of Easter. The lessons for the Sundays of Easter keep alive the fallout of the resurrection of our Lord to deepen our understanding of the presence of the Risen Christ among us and to point us forward with the hope we have because of the resurrection. We do not live after Easter. We live in the sure and solid hope of Easter.

I hope the sermons offered here will in some small way help to sharpen the focus of the second readings of Lent and Easter on the access we have to hope through our Lord Jesus Christ.

Lent Is About Reconciliation

The story of Lent really begins back in the Garden of Eden. The Passion of our Lord would not have been necessary if the creation and its creatures continued to exist in the state of bliss described as the condition of the origins of life. However, on Sunday, the First Sunday of Lent, the readings will include the tragic account of how sin entered into the world through the disobedience of the children of God. Some of us may recall having to read Milton's *Paradise Lost* back in first year of English in college. Or it may have been we had to read it in senior high. At any rate, Milton was convinced that the rehearsal of that story with proper interpretation would help all people to see that this was the root of all problems in the human condition. Above all, Milton wanted all his readers to understand that the Fall of Adam was the story of everyone.

Each person has to take responsibility for the subsequent judgment of his or her own rebellious behavior before God. It is obvious that the world has not given evidence of a common acknowledgment of Milton's insight. Yet the story of the Fall has its own final word. The story concludes with God giving promise that God will always war against the evil that had invaded the creation. At the same time, in order for people to look to God for help rather than the perfect creation as the creatures had, God closed down the perfect garden. The Cherubim was ordered to stand guard at the gate with the flaming sword. So it was that paradise was lost, and the rocky road we have to travel in life reminds us how the Cherubim stands between us and a rosy and smooth path in life.

A Rocky Road

Now mind you we have no evidence whatsoever that it was God's original intention to make life difficult for us. Rather, it is the other way around. The story of the Cherubim guarding the entrance into the garden with a flaming sword is meant to keep us from thinking that life consists only in living the life of Riley with complete ease. Life is not dependent upon our being comfortable! Our lives are totally dependent upon our relationship to God. The vision of the Cherubim with the fiery sword is designed to have us renounce any nostalgia for the Garden of Eden. We are to experience and discover our need to look to God. The creation itself manifests its warp without the perfection of the original garden. As the Apostle Paul says, "Creation was subjected to futility ... and the whole creation has been groaning in pain" (Romans 18:18-21). Thus it is not only that the creation has been scarred and marred by the occasion of the fall of humanity, but the creation itself appears to conspire against us.

In the Second Reading appointed for Ash Wednesday, the Apostle Paul gives an account of the obstacles he had to overcome in order to share the gospel with the people who comprised the congregation he had founded at Corinth. Paul had been especially careful to help the Corinthian Christians understand that the gospel had come to them completely free of charge. However, he also wanted them to understand that he had to pay a price in order for them to receive the gospel. He wrote, "No fault may be found with our ministry, but as servants of God we have commended ourselves in every way: through great endurance, in afflictions, hardships, calamities, beatings, imprisonments, riots, labors, sleepless nights, (and) hunger." All of us can identify with the majority of those experiences. We may not have been in prison or been in the midst of a riot, but we all flinch as we recall most of the other hardships and afflictions Paul mentioned. As he underwent these hardships in the pursuit of his calling, we do the same in our careers and vocations. As Willie Loman says in Arthur Miller's *Death Of A Salesman*, "It goes with the territory."

More Problems

It is true enough that we must suffer all kinds of problems that develop from a variety of sources. Some times we can identify the source of some of the hardships. Other times we cannot. In addition, people can make life difficult for us. Paul had his problems with the people in the congregation at Corinth. The two letters to the Church at Corinth may have been three or four letters, and he indicates that he had written more. The letters deal with the problems within the congregation. A good part of the difficulty was the attitude of some of the people toward Paul. His authority was called into question. Then some of the people also reacted poorly to some advice he had given. Once more we have a feeling that what went on with Paul was symptomatic of the same kind of problems we face from time to time in our human relations.

Paul mentions that some of the people held him in ill repute. Some claimed he was an impostor of the apostles. Some complained of his effectiveness because of his illnesses. Others wanted him punished. And the congregation at Corinth did not contribute to his support. Who has not known some of these criticisms? All of us have known those people who treat us shabbily. There are times when our paranoia is extremely acute because of the manner in which people treat us. Critics have commented on the fiftieth anniversary of the drama *Death Of A Salesman*. After fifty years the play still speaks to the American experience. In Willie Loman, the salesman, Arthur Miller caught the kind of pain that comes to people who fail in their human relations. It is the universal experience of hurt people feel when they have been ill treated by others, when they feel they have messed up their own lives, and when they do not know who they are.

Time For A Change

Paul wanted the relationship between himself and the people at Corinth to change. He made a strong appeal to them. This was the right moment for them to be reconciled to one another. Whenever things go bad between people, that is the time to do something about it. We should not wait. Paul quotes from the Prophet Isaiah (49:8), "At an acceptable time I have listened to you, and on a day of salvation I have helped you." Paul wanted the Corinthians to see that a practical application of their salvation was involved. They could make a current application of the faith in God's mercy by being merciful to one another. That certainly would be a wholesome application of the faith. Paul would want reconciliation to take place before the return of the Lord. However, why wait until the last minute? Isn't that true of all our human relations? If people delay the time of working out a reconciliation with someone, they have to carry the pain of anger and hurt around in their hearts, their heads, and their stomachs.

The anger, the hurt, and the desire for vengeance wear on us and eat away at us. If we think we can postpone reconciliation, we ought to take note of the fact that our irascibility literally shortens our lives, and we pay dearly for our anger. Paul's advice would be to deal with the problem and confront those who have hurt or wounded us so that we might deal with them. Yet we all know how difficult it is to make the first move toward reconciliation. There is always the feeling that we are giving up something, that we lose something. We think we are in danger of "losing face." No matter how reasonable it may appear at times that we should be reconciled to our neighbor, our emotions have their own logic which says that we cannot afford to give away something. That is the heart of the problem. Our emotions have their own rationale and their own demands. When that happens we rightfully say we are pathological. That is to say, we are reflecting the logic of how we feel.

There Is A Better Way

Paul would argue that there is a far better way for us to deal with damaged human relations. Instead of trying to rationalize our way through the matter or dealing with the logic of our emotions, we can deal with others on the same basis that God has dealt with us. Paul reminded the Corinthians that he had come to them as ambassador of our Lord Jesus Christ. That meant he was to preach and teach that God had reconciled the world unto himself through our Lord Jesus Christ. Because we are reconciled to God, we know how God did that for us. God made Jesus "to be sin for us who knew no sin, so that in him we might be made the righteousness of God." Therefore we are put in the position of being clean, of being pure, of being forgiven, of being established as the children of God. We are God's children regardless of what people have done to us or said about us, or how they have hurt us. We have the advantage of knowing that we are free to act toward our neighbor exactly the same way that God has acted toward us.

We can act in the freedom of grace. We can love, forgive, show mercy, or whatever is necessary for our neighbor to know that we see him or her in a perfectly new way. We can look at the neighbor in the same way that God looks at us. That is reconciliation. That is being reconciled, or being made friends again. In order to impress that upon ourselves and to equip ourselves to act by God's grace and mercy, we can go back again to that scene in the garden, where all the problems began. The Cherubim with the flaming sword has not reopened paradise for us. We cannot go back to that life of ease. However, all obstacles between God and us are removed. There is nothing to prevent us from accepting what God has offered to us through our Lord Jesus Christ.

No Obstacle

Paul stresses that there does not have to be any obstacle between him and the Corinthians, because God has healed the situation between God and us by moving all obstacles. We can do the same. Paul says to the Corinthians, "We are putting no obstacle in anyone's way, so that no fault may be found with our ministry, but as servants of God we have commended ourselves in every way." Then Paul goes on to mention all those things that he had endured for the sake of getting the word to the Corinthians in the first place. By the grace of God we can employ the same strategies in dealing with our neighbors who do us injury or harm. We began by noting that all of us have to travel a rocky road in life. Like the Apostle Paul we have to deal with all kinds of troubles. We do not need the added burdens of carrying around the pain our neighbors caused us or the resulting anger.

In his book *The Gift Of Peace*, Joseph Cardinal Bernardin made notes about his bout with cancer before his death. While he was serving as the Roman Catholic Archbishop of Chicago, the church and our nation was shocked when he was accused of having molested a seminarian when the archbishop had served in Cincinnati. The archbishop relates how difficult it was for him to handle this untrue allegation. However, during his illness he made the trip to Philadelphia to confront his accuser who was dying of AIDS. The accuser had dropped the charges against Bernardin, had given up the faith, and was no longer a member of the church. Bernardin forgave him and asked him to admit Bernardin had not abused him. The accuser complied. Bernardin also offered to say a mass for him. The accuser refused. Bernardin then offered a Bible as a gift. The accuser broke down and asked that a mass be said immediately. Reconciliation had taken place. The obstacles were removed because Christ had made reconciliation possible. Just so reconciliation in the worst of circumstances is always possible for us.

The Resources

The Apostle Paul would make it perfectly clear that when we are called to be ambassadors for Christ for the ministry of reconciliation, we are not merely being called to imitate what God has done for us. In one sense that should be motive enough, and we certainly are deeply moved by the fact that if God forgives our lives, we should be able to forgive a neighbor or neighbors. However, God has also filled us with the resources to be able to serve as reconcilers in the world. He indicates that he was able to deal with the tensions with the Corinthians "by purity, knowledge, patience, kindness, holiness of spirit, genuine love, truthful speech, and the power of God." Those are the gifts God gives us for dealing with human relations. We are not left to rely upon our own weaknesses and excuses for not being forgiving.

Richard Carlson, a psychiatrist, has written a book titled *Don't Sweat The Small Stuff*. The book was on the best seller list for months on end. It is written exceedingly well and is most appropriate for our generation which bitterly complains about stress. Of course, such a successful book had to have a sequel, which is, *Don't Sweat The Small Stuff At Work*. About the middle of the second book, the author writes, "Become Aware of Your Wisdom."

What Carlson writes is wholesome stuff for good mental and emotional health. However, this chapter epitomizes the approach. Carlson would have you make the most of what you have. The Apostle Paul helps you to go way beyond that. He encourages you to use the gifts of the Spirit, the gifts of God, which are the assurance that the power of God lives within you. The weakness of most therapy is that it relies on the resources of the flawed patient. Paul's offer of the Holy Spirit is an offer of God's resources.

A Final Word

Paul's advice worked. Paul and the Corinthian congregation were reconciled. As a result, we have the epistles he wrote to that congregation as models of how reconciliation works between Christians and how it can work between Christian and non-Christian or non-believer. We know also that sometimes this approach to reconciliation does not work. The majority of the world does not live by grace and forgiveness. That makes it all the more important for us who have been reconciled unto God to serve as the agents of reconciliation in the world. We started out by observing that the majority of the world does not understand the depths of the depravity in the world are caused by our disobedience to God. The story of the Fall in the garden of Eden should remind us of our own fallenness. The Cherubim with the flaming sword at the entrance to the garden of perfection was to be a reminder that we cannot look to the creation as a means of achieving the perfect life. Rather we must look to the Creator who does not disappoint us.

In the passion and death of our Lord Jesus Christ, God has removed all obstacles to life and peace with God. Nicolaus Herman, a hymn writer of the Reformation Era, could pen the Christmas hymn in which he wrote that our Lord Jesus Christ is the key and door to the new Paradise. "The angel guards the gate no more," he could write. We do not look back upon the first Paradise with any sense of longing. Now we can look forward to the relationship with God which has been perfected and made possible through the life, passion, death, and resurrection of our Lord Jesus Christ. Whatever obstacles have been thrown in our way by the demonic forces of the world we can overcome by faith and trust through which our Lord delivers us as authorized agents of God's grace and love for the reconciliation of the world. Our Lord Jesus Christ has made that possible for us. The Apostle Paul exemplified for us how it is done. This Lenten season is shaped to fill us anew with the power of that grace, love, and forgiveness to be reminded of how we are called to serve as reconcilers.

The Beginning Of It All

On May 20, 1927, Charles A. Lindbergh left New York on his solo flight to cross the Atlantic in his plane, the *Spirit of St. Louis*. The whole world waited with bated breath to hear if this brave young man could accomplish the feat that would introduce the infant airplane industry to a new era of world travel. The humorist Will Rogers wrote in his daily newspaper column that there would be no jokes that day. He noted it was a day when the young flier would be prayed for to every kind of supreme being who had a following. One newspaper columnist asked rhetorically if Lindbergh was flying alone? Hardly, he answered. He wrote that personified Courage, Skill, Ambition, and Adventure rode along in that plane. Beyond that, there were millions of people on both sides of the ocean who were with him. A. Scott Berg noted all of this along with much more in his lengthy and definitive biography of the remarkable personage of Charles Lindbergh.

Berg observed that when the humble young hero wrote an account of the flight in the book titled *We*, Lindbergh meant to include all of his sponsors, the manufacturers of the plane, the ground crew, and all the people who were his supporters. What a support system that was! The Lindbergh experience is an ideal example of how intimately our lives can become one. We can become united in the common experience of an event or through the special feats of one individual. In the Second Reading today, the Apostle Paul helps us to understand how we are all joined together through the experiences of both the First and the Second Adams.

All Have Sinned

Paul begins his essay on how we are all related through the experiences of the two Adams by rehearsing the significance of the First Adam. He writes, "Just as sin came into the world through one man." Paul in no way would suggest that when Adam and Eve sinned in the Garden of Eden, their disobedience demands that now all of humankind has the burden of paying for their sin. The reality is that sin did first come into the world through Adam, but sin comes into the world the same way every day since. The story of Adam's fall is our story. Sometimes people talk about original sin as though we inherited from Adam his sin. No, our sin is original with us. We sin originally. Paul says death came into the world as a result of sin, "and so death spread to all because all have sinned."

John Grisham pictures this for us in his novel *Testament*. Troy Phelan is a self-made billionaire, who has seven heirs whom he has sired through three wives. Phelan regards all those children, together with their mothers, as totally obnoxious. What Phelan has to reckon with is the fact that what makes the children so un-lovable are the same drives that made him what he was. They were all made of the same cloth. Their desires were the same. Nate Riley, a lawyer, is assigned to find another potential heir in the wilds of central Brazil. Nate, himself, is an alcoholic, a broken man who has lost count of how many times he has been through treatments for his drug abuse. This cast of characters illustrates how perva-sive the sin within the human condition is and how trapped all are by the same sin. Nate Riley comes to recognize painfully how desperate the human condition is, and that the cure itself cannot be found within oneself. Help has to come from beyond one's self. This hard fact about humankind is universal. As Paul points out, "Death spread to all because all have sinned." All human beings are as linked together by their sin as they are linked together by their common ancestry. As surely as we are the children of Adam, we are all the children of sin and death.

Adam As Type

Paul wants everyone to understand the direct connection be-tween sin and death. Death did come as the result of sin. He knows sin was in the world before the Law. There was no formal law before Adam sinned in the Garden of Eden. The Law of God as we know it was not in its formal form before Moses. Paul mentions this, because ordinarily one does not count something as sin unless there is a law prohibiting it. Yet death was very much in the world before Moses came along. Death also came to people whose sin was not like the sin of Adam. This had great significance for Paul. What it meant for Paul was that Adam, the first one to sin, became a "type of the one who was to come." Paul uses the term "type" here in a unique way. The Greek word is τυποζ which comes from a Greek word τυπτο, which means "to strike." One would strike with a hollow mold so as to make a similar thing.

In Paul's time the word τυποζ was used as a "model." Paul does use the word that way sometimes or as to express something as "typical" (cf. 1 Corinthians 10:1 and 11). Here, however, he uses the word as a universal experience. Adam is a type of the one who is to come in the sense that as surely as sin and death were to be identified with all of humankind with the havoc Adam introduced to the world, so the life of the Second Adam would be the universal benefit of humankind. In that sense the sin and death of Adam are a preview of what would happen with the coming of the Second Adam. The second universal experience would be of a higher nature and would be the opposite of the first experience. What is typical about the experience is that universally we participate in both.

Death Exercised Dominion

There is no escaping the fact that, as Paul indicated, death exercised dominion after the fall of humankind. Death stalks all of life. Death intimidates us, and death controls all of life. The list of things we do to prevent death is endless. We do so in taking preventative measures to insulate ourselves against violence. We do what we must to prevent accidents. We adopt medicinal, physical, and dietary practices to postpone death. We are doing an extremely good job of that. The average life span has been increased considerably in recent years. To sense that, all one has to do is pick up the morning newspaper to read the obituaries. It is not a surprise to see the high ages people have achieved. A good number of the listings are people who have achieved the eighties and the nineties. We are no longer shocked to read summaries of the lives of people who have reached a hundred and more years.

Futurists note the possibility that people will soon stretch their lives to 150 years, not only because of our expertise in diagnostics and exotic surgeries but because of the rise in the use of vitamin and health supplements. Yet the fact remains that death is still the last enemy. What is important is not only that we exercise the best physical and hygienic regimes to fight off the threats to physical health, but that we know that we are fighting also the threat to our spiritual well-being. Death is the enemy because it is the result of our sinful condition, not simply a weakened physical condition. That is the emphasis that the Apostle Paul would make in alerting us to recognize the human condition common to us all. Long, long ago someone coined the phrase that the only two sure things in life are death and taxes. No doubt the originator of the saying was more worried at the moment about taxes and how to avoid them. Paul would have us be more concerned about the implications and significance of our common experience of death as the result of sin. At the same time Paul helps us to understand what God has done to reverse the result of the human condition.

The Free Gift

Paul writes it should be obvious to us that all humans die from the time that sin entered into the world by one man's trespass. What is not so obvious to all people is that now the grace of God comes wrapped as a free gift in the grace of one man, Jesus Christ. We are not used to that. We can readily see how all people sin like Adam. Nobody is perfect. Yet it is hard to see that everyone receives the free gift. Not everyone wins the lottery. Not everyone wins in the *Reader's Digest* or magazine sweepstakes. Billie Letts has written a novel about a seventeen-year-old pregnant, unmarried girl titled *Where The Heart Is*. Novalee Nation is left abandoned and totally depressed in a small town in Oklahoma. Yet a quartet of caring people come to her rescue. A religious older woman, an older African-American, the son of an aristocratic family, and a young native American combine to make everything come up roses for Novalee.

When Billie Letts was interviewed about her novel, she mentioned that there were all kinds of young unmarried mothers in Oklahoma who suffered the same kind of abandonment as Novalee. Billie wanted more people to care about them. The truth is that the majority of the abandoned young mothers do not have the same kind of free gifts coming to them as Novalee did. Free gifts normally are not delivered evenly. However, Paul makes the point that the free gift in Jesus Christ is for all people. Paul writes, "If, because of the one man's trespass, death exercised dominion through that one, much more surely will those who receive the abundance of grace and the free gift of righteousness exercise dominion in life through the one man, Jesus Christ."

Justification For All

The effect of what Paul has to say about the manner in which Jesus Christ, the Second Adam, brought grace and light into the world is to reverse completely the effect of what came into the world by the First Adam. As the First Adam opened the door to sin and death, the Second Adam broke into life with righteousness and life. The result is that death no longer has to hold sway over everything we do and say. The bumper sticker on the truck of the carpet man says, "Life is short. Pray a lot." The intention, of course, is a holy effort to get the tailgater to think of how death makes life a short span in which one is accountable. The free gift of life and righteousness Jesus brings makes a different emphasis. In Christ we know that life is eternal. We are free to serve now with the confidence that what we do in service to others is righteous and endures in love and grace to eternity. That may not be apparent to everyone, and that is the point. By faith we know that what we do in love is not measurable by worldly standards.

Our lives are not measured by calendars, ratios, judgments, guidelines, or any other kind of yardsticks. Our lives are already redeemed, that is, forgiven and made holy, and made fit for eternity. That is what Paul means when he summarizes, "Just as one man's trespass led to condemnation for all, so one man's act of righteousness leads to justification for all. For just as by the one man's disobedience the many were made sinners, so by the one man's obedience the many will be made righteous." Paul goes on in the next breath to say, "Where sin increased, grace abounded all the more." Faith recognizes that in a way that the world cannot understand apart from the revelation that God has made in Jesus Christ. This says, no matter how bad it is in the world, internationally, nationally, locally, or personally, God is covering for us. That is not to say, God is covering up the situation, but rather God gives us the freedom to act, to cope, to intervene to do what we can to alter matters and know that results are already forgiven or counted as righteous.

Life Is Free For All

President John Kennedy is quoted frequently for his observation that life is not fair. He, of course, used the expression to indicate how difficult it is to govern and let people think that life will be the same or fair for all people. Observers, however, could relate Mr. Kennedy's statement about life to the successive misfortunes that happened to the Kennedy family. This is an American family the nation has watched with great interest, because few American families have known so much wealth, power, and fame. Yet their propensity for tragedian pains and losses modeled for Americans how fragile all of life, fame, and fortune are. Glumly Senator Ted Kennedy observed, "There are more of us than there is trouble." That was one way to accept or cope with the list of Kennedy calamities. However, the witness to the faith was more in evidence than that.

Yet Jack Kennedy's word about life being unfair did not originate with him. All parents should know that they have to teach their children that. Woe to them if they do not know that! It is impossible to make life come out fair for your children. And it is extremely difficult to help understand how life is not fair. We all struggle with that in our lives. When misfortune or pain come to us, we wonder why we have to be the target. When we are passed over or passed by, we are pained. On and on it goes. Why me?

Why not me? Our Lord lifts the burdens from trying to make life fair under the terms of any earthly or legal judgments. He makes it possible to live under the freedom of grace and love which lift us above making life fair to take what comes with the freedom of grace and divine patience.

God Does It All

Ernest Gaines has written a novel that partially illustrates what Paul has written in this text from Romans. The novel, *A Lesson Before Dying,* is set in the South in the '40s. Jefferson is an African-American who has been condemned to the electric chair for a murder he did not commit. In the courtroom, his defender offered what appeared to be an impassioned plea in order to win the compassion of the jury. He said the jury should not want to send this hog to its death in the electric chair. Jefferson's godmother Emma knows that she could never work for a reprieve for Jefferson. However, she knows how depressed he is not only for the injustice but the greater judgment that he is no more than a hog. Emma approaches Grant Wiggins, a teacher of children, to work with Jefferson to assure him that he is not a hog and that he can go to his death as a man. Wiggins is reluctant but gives in. He does not belong to the church and does not think of himself as a believer. After struggling with Jefferson and trying to give him strength, Wiggins finally begins to rely on the language of the faith he thought he had given up. Jefferson responds to that. He goes to the chair standing tall as a man and a child of God. Someone asks Wiggins how he did it. Wiggins replies that he did not do it. Who then? Wiggins surprises himself and his questioner by saying that God did it. That is how it is for us, too.

Only God is the One who is able to prepare us for the death that comes upon us. God handles what no one else can. There is pseudepigrapha material, that is, writing which pretends to be authored by an historic person, which makes Eve out to be the real temptress in the Garden of Eden, excusing Adam from being the first to fall from grace. There always will be someone trying to escape the fault for sin and death entering our lives. Paul helps us to see that we are all in it together, caught up in the same guilt and death with Adam. However, by the grace and mercy of God we are also by faith caught up into the life, death, and resurrection of our Lord Jesus Christ so that in the Christ we are made both alive and righteous. From the beginning the promise of release from sin and death was promised in him. In him we are set free.

Abraham, Our Father

Abraham is the central character in the First and Second Readings appointed for today. The Apostle Paul calls Abraham "the father of us all," which is the theme of a thought-provoking book by Karl-Josef Kuschel. Kuschel is a professor of ecumenical theology at the University of Tuebingen. The title of the book is *Abraham: Sign Of Hope For Jews, Christians And Muslims.* The book is an appeal to peoples of the three great religions to search their heritage to understand how Abraham should be a common point of reference for them. That is most important in a world of hostility in which the tensions between the peoples of the three religions are intensified with increases of fundamentalism and extremism. Kuschel demonstrates how Abraham, a Chaldean, was made a Jew by the Jews. Then Christians made Abraham a Christian. The Muslims counted Abraham a model Muslim.

Instead of each religion claiming Abraham exclusively, it is important that they recognize that within their own traditions Abraham is regarded as being hospitable to all peoples. It would be on the basis of their commonality that the three religions could explore future relationships and overcome the hostilities and prejudices that separate them. While each religion would most certainly keep their special identities, each would also find in Abraham an openness and inspiration for negotiations for peace. Kuschel calls his program "An Abrahamic Ecumenism." The Roman Catholic Hans Kung and the Egyptian Anwar Sadat were very much attracted to his proposal. Certainly the Apostle Paul left room for that kind of negotiation in his understanding of Abraham.

Abraham, The Chaldean

The First Reading today is a brief account of how the call came from God to Abraham originally. As usual there are those scholars who would say that the existence of an historical Abraham is questionable. However, the traditions surrounding him are so well developed as to make the theory of a non-historical Abraham out of the question. At the same time, we do not have any way of discovering at what precise date the call from God came to him. Nor do we have any way in which we can establish how it was that Abraham made the move from the Ur of the Chaldees to Mesopotamia. We are told that his father Terah took Abraham and his daughter-in-law Sarah to go into Canaan. However, when they got to Haran, they stayed there, and Abraham's father died there. It was then that Abraham received a word from God that he should go unto Canaan (Genesis 12:1-2). How that word was delivered to him we do not know.

Jimmy Carter tells us that he got the word to run for the presidency of the United Sates of America one day when he was sitting at poolside in Atlanta. He had a similar impulse to run for the governorship of Georgia and won. He felt he had served well as a governor and could do the same as president of his nation. He looked over the field of candidates and felt he could do better than any of them. He felt called to do so. Did Abraham go through a similar kind of reasoning? Did he decide that the idols that he and his family had been worshiping in the Land of Chaldea did nothing for him? The book of Joshua said that he had been an idolater (Joshua 24:2). Did he become a monotheist because it just made good sense to disown the kind of problems idolatry created and also failed to solve? The tradition and stories about him suggest that possibility. He is pictured as a wise and sensitive judge of human nature, a good administrator of great wealth, and an extremely devout man.

Idealizing Abraham

Two Jewish historians did their best to establish the fact that Abraham was a model of faith for all the world. The two historians were Philo and Josephus, contemporaries of Jesus. Philo was born to wealth in Alexandria, one of the centers of Grecian culture. Philo made the effort to demonstrate that Abraham was a world citizen. As a Chaldean, Abraham was not a Jew but a Gentile. He was a model believer with a faith in the Creator of the universe. As such, he was a model of faith and reconciliation within the Hellenistic or Grecian culture. The other historian, Josephus, was born to a wealthy family in Jerusalem. He, too, emphasized the fact that Abraham, a non-Jew, became the progenitor of Israel. Josephus was taken to Rome as a prisoner, but ended up in the court of the Emperor Vespasian as one of the emperor's favorites.

Josephus did his best to demonstrate that Abraham arrived at his monotheism through philosophical and scientific observations of the creation or nature. Because of these scientific and spiritual insights Abraham also highly influenced culture. Josephus noted that when Abraham was in Egypt, he introduced astronomy and arithmetic to the Egyptians. For Josephus, Abraham represented the best in social and learned behavior. In the Roman Empire of his day, Josephus was bent on demonstrating how the faith of the conquered people of Israel could speak to the most sophisticated and learned people of the empire. Both Philo and Josephus did their best to explain the faith of Abraham as reasonable and philosophical results from the observations of nature. Both make much of the fact that Abraham observed much ritual, spiritual, and social behavior which had not yet been formulated as the Hebraic or Jewish code.

Luther's View
Martin Luther had problems with any efforts to demonstrate that faith is born out of our own reason. Though he was highly appreciative of the work of the philosophers who wrestled with the questions of the universe, he disqualified them for their efforts to describe God. We do not come to faith in the true God apart from revelation. As Paul says, people by nature do not discern the spiritual things of God. At the same time Luther had trouble with people who claimed a direct revelation from God by the Spirit. He called them the Schwaermerei, the "enthusiasts," people who, he said, swallowed the Holy Spirit, "feathers and all." So Luther had

trouble with Abraham. How did God come to him? How did the word, the call, come to him from God? Luther was convinced that the word had to be ministered to him. Someone had to instruct him and inform him.

Luther took a hard look at the table of the generations in the eleventh chapter in Genesis. He calculated from that material that Abraham was a contemporary of Shem, a son of Noah. Luther surmises that it was Shem who was the preacher or teacher for the idolater Abraham. It is either Shem or someone whom Shem sends to Abraham to bring him to repentance, to disown his idols, and to embrace faith in God. That certainly is a wild guess on the part of Luther. However, it does represent his conviction that God had not left God without witness in the primitive records we have about the beginnings of the very faith which we espouse. God does have to work through people. God relies upon people to make the witness. That had to be true when God dealt with Abraham. What is so striking about the call to Abraham is that God calls an idolater. The call is unmistakable, however. The call is radical in its demands. In order to know, appreciate, and believe what God intends for Abraham he must leave his homeland, his relatives, and his father's house. It were as though the word was that if Abraham remained where he was, he would not be saved. He had to be separated from his former way of life.

Paul's Concern

Since the call of God did come to Abraham in such a dramatic form, the tendency is to focus on the obedience of Abraham as a great act or deed. Perhaps most of us in this highly mobile age know what is demanded of us when we are called upon to make a move. It could be downsizing, a merger, or a failure in business that may necessitate having to make a move. Or it could be a challenge through a career change, upgrading a position, or an offer to new leadership that could call for a move. Such changes call for a total review of one's situation, family obligations, and community involvement. The whole family might have to work at making a final decision whether one should leave one's present environs to take on the new position. We certainly would see that as work. On the other hand, there are moves that people make without having to give much thought or work as to whether one should move. If the environment itself becomes a threat, one does not have to think much about making the move. We know of communities that have been disturbed by pollution or radiation. Some have been threatened by erosion. Others may have been disturbed by social problems, such as a drug culture. In those instances the decision to move has been made for them.

Abraham's call begins on an emergent note. The decision has been made for him. He must move beyond the idolatrous culture and home in which he has been living. It was the Apostle Paul who wanted people to understand this most clearly. Both Jewish and Gentile Christians should understand that the initiative for Abraham's calling came from God. It was by grace that God came to deliver Abraham from his environment to begin life anew under the promises of God. Paul does not mention an Hebraic tradition about Abraham which says that Abraham was thrown into a fire, because of his protest of Chaldean idolatry. Paul may not have known of that tradition which adds that Abraham was saved because of his protest. If Paul did know about it, he would not have counted it as a work of salvation for Abraham. Paul uses Abraham as a prime model of how people are saved by grace.

Not By Works

Paul is most explicit in saying that works had nothing to do with Abraham's standing before God. It was in this essay Paul wrote to the congregation at Rome that Paul wanted to teach as clearly as possible how it is that people are saved. Paul was not only aiming at legalistic religion insisting that we make ourselves acceptable to God by our piety and our works. Paul knew that to be a normal and natural tendency. We are filled with the urge to please others in order to be liked. We constantly ask ourselves how we are doing. Paul makes note of that. In the world the pattern is "to one who works, wages are not reckoned as a gift but as something due."

In the world you have a right to expect payment for your wages and boast about it. You can even ask for a raise if you think you deserve it and are bold enough to do so. However, do not try that with God. In the first place, you have not done enough or done well enough to merit God's approval. Paul handled that in the previous section in which he showed how we all fall short of the glory of God. However, here the emphasis is on the fact that God does not establish relationship with us through the law or works. What God does is make an offer of love and grace that is too good to refuse. The story about Abraham is about promise and faith. The promise God made to Abraham was that he "would inherit the world," says Paul. Now that kind of promise did not come by the law. For if it did, Abraham and his descendants would have been wiped out, for the law could only condemn idolaters. On top of that, if people become heirs of the world by law, then "faith is null and the promise is void," says Paul.

Counted As Righteous

Paul points out that in Abraham's case the promise was both valid and effective. God promised Abraham that he would be the father of a great nation and in him all the nations of the earth would be blessed. What a promise! Why wouldn't Abraham bite on that? Yet he did have to leave his homeland, culture, and relatives. He did have to believe that he would be a father. Yet there were no signs of fatherhood being very likely in his case. He already was very old, and his wife Sarah was barren. Time was passing him by. The years passed into decades, and still Abraham had no heir. God was willing to renew the promise to Abraham. With no heir, Abraham offered the suggestion that he make a steward in his home his legal heir. God vetoed that proposal. Instead God assured Abraham that he would have his own heir. Then God suggested that Abraham look at the sky to count the stars if he was able, because his descendants would be that numerous. Abraham believed God, and the writer says, "And the Lord reckoned it to him as righteousness" (Genesis 15:6).

The writer noted that God now looked upon Abraham, the sinful idolater, as righteous. The one who had been committed to a life of worshiping idols and living life on those terms is now regarded by God as one who is God's righteous and holy child, a son

30

of God. It was all by faith. Abraham had not lifted a hand to make this a possibility. Paul says with good reason it depends on faith, in order that the promise may rest on grace and be guaranteed to all his descendants, to those who share the faith of Abraham. Paul says this promise includes us. Abraham is "the father of us all." Paul says we believe in the same God as Abraham. It is the God "who gives life to the dead and calls into existence the things that do not exist."

The Offer Is Universal

Paul's application of this truth about the faith of Abraham was to help both the Jewish and Gentile Christians in the congregation at Rome to know that they were made one, or united, by their common faith in the Lord Jesus Christ. They believed that the promise given to Abraham came to its fulfillment, was incarnate in the person of Jesus, and was played out in the life, death, and resurrection of our Lord Jesus Christ. Jesus could say that Abraham had seen his day and believed in it (John 8:56). In this Lententide we concentrate on the meaning of the Passion of our Lord. We would not be able to understand that, if we did not know about the history of salvation God had initiated with the faith God created beginning with Abraham. Nor could we understand the benefits of the Passion of our Lord as extended to us if it were not offered to all. That is the clincher for Paul.

Paul draws out the fact that though the promise was given to Abraham, it was intended to be passed on and extended to all. Paul quotes again from Genesis, "I have made you the father of many nations" (Genesis 17:4). As it is, the promise is universal. In the later chapters of Romans, Paul points out that the promise of God and the Covenant of God had never been revoked as far as the Jews are concerned. Therefore they can still be saved if they share in the faith of Abraham in the promise of God. We began by noting that Karl-Josef Kuschel has proposed that Jews, Christians, and Muslims could find commonality in the faith they have come to know through Abraham. He called it an "Abrahamic ecumenism." Paul helped us to understand that to be true if we are talking about faith in God that is shaped alone by the promise of God as we know it in Christ Jesus. We would scuttle any proposal that suggests one must add elements of law and fulfillment of the law that makes null and void faith and the promise. However, we welcome all who can confess that, like Abraham, we are saved by faith without the deeds of the law.

Access To Grace

One of the most colorful, exciting, and stirring scenes in all of the scriptures is the call of the prophet Isaiah. The account is dated in the year that King Uzziah died. That does not necessarily mean Uzziah was already dead. This scene could have taken place in the temple during a religious festival such as New Year's Day. At such a festival, the cultic ceremonies honored the divine king being enthroned as conqueror of all the enemies of the people. Either at the time of such a ceremony, or in the fresh memory of it, Isaiah, a young priest, had a splendid vision in which he sensed the presence of the Almighty God surrounded by seraphim, the angels who were attendants in the heavenly court of God. The seraphim dialogued with one another with booming voices which shook the threshold of the temple and filled the place with smoke.

Isaiah sensed the irony of the situation. Here he was a sinful man witnessing the presence of God. He confessed his inadequacy and sinfulness in the presence of angelic antiphonal choruses chanting about the holiness and glory of God. With that, one the seraphim was dispatched to take a hot coal from the altar of sacrifice and touch the lips of the frightened Isaiah to cleanse him and make him fit for the prophetic office to which God called him. How many times has not every one of us longed for a moment when God would make the divine presence felt and send an angel to touch us on the shoulder with an answer to our prayer for help? How handy it would be if the angels could be at our beck and call when we feel the pressure to come up with answers. In the pain of our loneliness and emptiness, it would be most helpful if we could rely on the touch from an angel.

The Need For Grace

The truth of the matter is that when we get to that moment when we would like very much to have God dispatch an angel to us, like Isaiah, we feel a dreadful inadequacy. We wonder if that is not the reason we do not get an answer in the first place. Henry Kissinger wrote of that kind of moment in his book *Years of Upheaval*. He described that painful last night of Richard Nixon's presidency when the president knew that impeachment was imminent if he did not resign. Nixon remembered that he asked Kissinger to kneel and pray with him. Kissinger says he cannot recall whether he knelt or not. However, he did recall that he was filled with such a deep sense of awe that he did not know exactly what to pray for. He said a passage from one of the Greek tragedies of Aeschylus kept running through his mind: "Pain that cannot forget / falls drop by drop / upon the heart / until in our despair / there comes wisdom / through the awful grace of God."

Despair is what we must experience first before we can discover the "awful" grace of God. That is what Paul writes about in the Letter to the Romans. It is while we "were weak" Christ died for the ungodly. It is in the death of the Lord Jesus Christ that God gave the abundant proof that God loves us while we are still sinners. In Christ, God reconciled us unto God. It is in that act of reconciliation that God changed our situation for us and gave us a whole new approach to life as well as to the problems in life. What this means is that by making us friends with God, God has removed all the barriers that would stand between us and God. God made us authentic beings again so that we can live honestly before God and with ourselves. We can remove from our minds and hearts any fear or question we might have about God's willingness to help and defend us. God restored to us the kind of privileges that God intended God's creatures to have in the first place. Having been saved from the wrath of God, in Christ we discover we can afford to be ourselves, that is, the kind of people who know their lives came from God and are completely dependent upon God.

Peace With God

Because we have been reconciled to God, because we are justified by our Lord Jesus Christ through his suffering and death for us, Paul says we have peace with God. Paul rushes on to say that this peace is not completely passive, that is, simply that we do not have to stop worrying about our relationship with God. The peace we enjoy with God opens to us many advantages. The chief of these is that now "we have obtained access to this grace in which we stand." We literally have access to God. We have an inside track. To have an access to authority is most helpful. One time in Chicago the mayor and the city council were at an impasse. The city was suffering from the lack of services. It was then that the president of the Chicago Church Federation, the Roman Catholic archbishop, and a rabbi met with the mayor and the chief obstructionist in the city council. By conferring with the city officials the clergy were able to develop agreements that put the city back to work.

The clergy had access to the authority. We know how that works in business. Someone is on a job search and looks for the people who can give the job seeker access to the powers that be. We know how that works in the home. The children learn very quickly how to find access to the parent or parents who will give them help. What is so notable about the access Paul says we have to God is that this is access to grace, grace in which we already stand. We do not have to fear the authority as being neutral or hostile toward us. This is access to grace which is already expressed in love for us. It is grace in which we stand. We already have favor in God's sight. We begin with God on our side.

A Share In Glory

Paul expands on the advantages we have because we have been justified by grace through our Lord Jesus Christ. He writes, "And we boast in our hope of sharing the glory of God." That is like saying that we not only have access to God's grace, but that we can be all the more sure that we have God on our side. We are a part of the divine family. It is one thing for us to have access to God, but we know also that our future is secure with God. That is the hope that is ours, because as our Lord Jesus Christ was raised from the dead, we are confident that we will also share eternity with God. That was very important to the Apostle Paul. Over and over again Paul alludes to the fact that at the end, what in Greek he called the eschaton, we will be with God. That colors everything for us. Our lives are shaped by the fact that everything turns out okay for us.

Life is not a mystery story for us. We do not have to keep reading on to find out how the mystery will turn out. We already know what the ending will be. We will share in the glory of God. Because we know how the ending will turn out, we can handle the in-between stuff. That by no means suggests that the in-between stuff is not important. On the contrary, it suggests that we now have the freedom to handle everything in the light of our future glory with God. We give meaning to the in-between stuff. If you are the number one basketball team in the country, you still have to play through the Final Four to get to be number one. And you have to believe in yourselves to play well enough to get there. In our status with God, we know that we will make our goal, but we believe in God in order to get there. The difference is that we can also believe in ourselves because we share the place with God. We do not believe in ourselves because we are self-made in terms of our spiritual capability, but because God made us able to serve in grace and love in the way God served us. But we are the ones who serve. God uses us. We not only benefit from God's goodness, but we are enabled to serve out of goodness.

Boast In Suffering

Paul goes on to say that our privileges as people who have been justified by grace through our Lord Jesus Christ enable us also to boast in our sufferings. That is like punching a hole in the drum. First Paul says we have access to a gracious and loving God. Then he writes that we are to share in the glory of God. Now he says we can boast in our suffering. One would think that if we have access to the grace of God, and if we will share in the glory of God, we would escape suffering. That is not the way it is. We will all have to suffer one way or another. We do not have to go out of our way to experience suffering. That will come soon enough. We do not have to become self-styled martyrs. We all know people who react badly to suffering. We tire of the moaners and groaners. They are the people who think that suffering should come to everyone else but them. They act as though they are surprised that they should have to suffer. The other kind of people who boast about how much they have to suffer are a pain, too. They act as though pain is God-sent and that they can glory in pain. That all sounds artificial and makes God the source of pain. That is hard to swallow.

Well, what then does Paul mean when he says we should boast in our sufferings? From everything else Paul wrote about this, we gather he means we can suffer for the sake of the gospel as the children of God. We suffer for the sake of others. We suffer for the sake of the creation. Paul made long catalogues of what he had to suffer for the sake of the gospel. He boasts about that, not for his own glory, but because the cause of the gospel was served. It is a matter of being partners with God in whatever it takes to serve God's creation and creatures. Moreover, in our suffering we can identify with our Lord Jesus Christ who suffered death for our sakes. We know how Jesus did that without complaint but with the certainty that it would help us.

Endurance

There is a definite sense in which the church, that is, the people of God, is to suffer for the sake of the world. As Jesus came into the world for the sake of saving the world through his suffering and death, so the church is called to continue the mission of suffering on behalf of the world. Paul began this discussion by announcing we have peace through our Lord Jesus Christ. When the Christmas angels sang about peace on Bethlehem's plain, they were announcing that the one who came to bring peace upon the earth was coming into the world to suffer for the sake of the world. It may sound rather frightening when we say that Christians are supposed to pick up the suffering for the world where Christ left off. Paul, would say, "No!" Suffering as we experience it in Christ produces positive results. For one thing suffering "produces endurance," Paul says.

We know that everyone in the world suffers somehow. However, by faith through our Lord Jesus Christ we learn how to suffer. Our suffering produces the kind of endurance that is meaningful and has purpose. Not only when we suffer or sacrifice for the sake of the gospel, but also when we cope with any other kind of suffering, we endure the suffering in the light of our faith. Suffering in our lives becomes the occasion to be drawn close to God, because we know that God is present in suffering. It is the exact opposite for the world. The world believes their gods are absent when suffering comes. We find God at the cross in all suffering, so we know we can endure suffering with God present. When the suffering comes, we know that God comes. God is there to strengthen us and to hold us in the arms of divine mercy. For us our suffering is the sign God could not be closer. It is for us to look to God to give us the strength and the courage to endure in faith in God's love. That is how we boast in our suffering, by endurance in faith.

Character

Paul goes on to say that as we are able to cope with and endure suffering by our faith in the Lord Jesus Christ our endurance produces character. The death of the baseball player Joe DiMaggio produced all kinds of analysis of him as the great Yankee Clipper. All those who commented on him could speak of him as a great player with good statistics, who played with uncommon grace. He played at the game so diligently that he made every play look easy. However, it also is true there were other players greater than he. What endeared him so much to the sports world was his character. It was not only how he carried himself, but his demeanor and his conversation that made his character a standout in baseball history. Those who analyzed his game and eulogized his person could say he had character, because he played the game for the spectators and not for himself.

It is noteworthy that those who commented on the life of a baseball player could surmise that character is built out of selfless behavior. That is the kind of point that the Apostle Paul was making for the manner in which the Christian understanding of faith enables the believers to endure suffering so as to produce character. Believers can endure what they must as suffering for the sake of the gospel. They can also endure personal loss or suffering. Whenever they endure suffering, believers give witness to their character as the children of God. The believers are strengthened in their own faith as they endure and cope with suffering. In the very act of their being strengthened for suffering they might help others.

The Bottom Line

We began by noting the experience of Isaiah in the temple was highly privileged. It was an angelic scene in which angels guaranteed the presence of God, so Isaiah could say that a mere mortal had the privilege of seeing God. The crowning glory of that scene was an angel touching the lips of Isaiah with a coal to purify him for the role of the prophetic office. In the Epistle of Paul to the Romans we learned Isaiah was not any more privileged than we. We cannot say enough about the fact that through our Lord Jesus Christ we have direct access to the Father. Our reconciliation to God the Father through our Lord Jesus Christ puts us into the new position of being able to share in the glory of God, to endure suffering that ultimately produces character in us.

When Paul describes the benefits which accrue to us by faith in our Lord Jesus Christ, he talks about the hope that is in us. Paul adds, "And hope does not disappoint us." This is not like the disappointment people experience when they buy tickets for the lottery or enter the sweepstakes sponsored by the magazine distributors. Those are idle hopes with odds that are out of sight. No, Paul could say the hope we have within us "does not disappoint us, because God's love has been poured into our hearts through the Holy Spirit that has been given to us." This is no long shot that we are taking. This is talk about the reality of how God works in the lives of people. "God has poured his love into our hearts," says Paul. It is not as though God teases us with a little bit of information or holds out a carrot for us. God has done in Christ Jesus what should make us feel and know we are loved with an everlasting love to survive the worst of situations. Christ made it all real, because by his life, suffering, and death we gained access to the grace of God, and we gained the sure hope of sharing the glory of God.

Live In The Light

Sidney Sheldon repeatedly has given us evidence of his remarkable gift for weaving tales of the bizarre behavior of humanity bent on satisfying the self. His novel *Tell Me Your Dreams* involves a reach into what creates serious complications within the human mind and heart. David Singer, a young lawyer, is in conversation with Dr. Royce Salem, a psychiatrist. The case they are discussing is the person of a suspected serial killer, a client whom the lawyer is defending. Dr. Salem confesses that he had been especially fascinated by patients who have manifested multiple personality disorders. In fact, he had built a reputation for being able to help such persons.

The doctor explains to the lawyer that in reality we all have alter egos. He gives as examples the kind person who commits unexpected acts of cruelty and the cruel persons who can do very kind things. The doctor observes that *Dr. Jekyll And Mr. Hyde* is pure fiction, but it is based on fact. We can understand Dr. Salem. We all know how at times we struggle with confused emotions and strange impulses. Today in the Second Reading from the Epistle to the Ephesians we hear an apostolic word as an appeal for us to make concerted efforts to deal with those struggles within ourselves in a positive fashion. The word is, "Once you were darkness, but now in the Lord you are light. Live as children of the light."

You Were Darkness

This word from the Letter to the Ephesians was intended for the entire Christian community, for all the churches around the

41

Mediterranean. Scholars have never concluded the debate as to whether the Apostle Paul or someone after him wrote the letter. The argument against Pauline authorship is that some of the vocabulary appears alien to Paul. However, it could well be that Paul developed this letter in different terms, because he was not addressing problems that were peculiar to the congregations to which he had written. However, the authorship is not that important. What is important is to listen to the message which is definitely Pauline in character.

In this letter the writer describes the Christian experience that is common to all believers in Christ, how these common experiences unite them as one in Christ, and how they are to live in the Lord as the created new community within the old creation. One of the basic assumptions of the letter is that we recognize all Christian believers understand that they are also sinners. Not only are they sinners, but once they "were darkness." That is to say, they lived in a condition in which they did not understand the true nature of their sin, they did not recognize their sin as an estrangement from God, they did not know how to overcome their sin, and they did not know they did not have the power to overcome sin. That is the universal condition of humanity untouched by the grace and mercy of God. We can call it spiritual blindness or spiritual death. The word in the text is "you were darkness." Or we can say we simply were in the dark about ourselves. The human condition gets headlined regularly as we read and hear how perverse people can be. For us who were in the dark, we should be able to recognize that such behavior really is normal, because of the natural state of humanity. We should never be shocked at the enormity of the dreadful deviations in human behavior, because they are perpetrated by people still in the dark.

Now You Are The Light

A good expression of what it is to live in the dark is a confession to her friend by Kinsey Millhone, the private investigator in Sue Grafton's *M Is For Malice*. Kinsey complains she has been depressed for weeks. When Robert Dietz asks her to explain her depression she tells him she wonders what we are doing on this planet. Reports in the newspapers are hopeless. Poverty and disease are rampant. Politicians are unbelievable. The hole in the ozone and the destruction of rain forests create more anxiety that there is no order in the creation. All that is enough to make one wonder where one fits in, and one has to struggle for answers. To live in that kind of darkness is not to know about oneself. Then the problems of the creation, the society are emphasized and enlarged, because one senses that one's own person is as insoluble as the problems of the universe.

In contrast to such lack of understanding the self, we know who we are. Paul says in the Lord we are children of light. We know who we are in the Lord, because in Jesus Christ we know how God cares about us. Our identity is revealed in Christ. In him we can acknowledge what sinners we are, what spiritual buffoons we are, and how helpless we are. However, we also know in Jesus Christ our lives are precious, ransomed, and made righteous through the forgiveness of sins won for us by the life, death, and resurrection of our Lord Jesus Christ. To live in the light is to know that. It is to know that we can live in the world under the judgment of God and tormented by the sins of people. Yet we know that God brings us through it all to the perfection of eternity. We do fit in.

The Fruit Of The Light

We have the benefit of living in the light so that we can understand who we are and where we fit in the universe with its awesome wonder and frightening forces. Paul says, because we are the light, we should now "live as children of the light." He goes on to say what that involves. He writes, "For the fruit of the light is found in all that is good and right and true." The philosophers through the ages have been scratching their heads and rattling their brains to discover what is "good and right and true." For Paul what is "good and right and true" God reveals as "good and right and true." We do not manufacture, discover, or uncover the "good and right and true." No matter how beautiful, exact, and honest we may find something in the creation, in our own inventions, or in the arts, apart from the relation to God it ends as dry rot for us.

Back to Sue Grafton's *M Is For Malice,* Guy Malek is a missing person Kinsey Millhone is hired to find. When she finds him he explains the reasons for his wild and lost youth. He admits that his parents were good people. They did not abuse him and cared for him, but they never talked about God. He was raised without a moral compass, rudderless and unable to solve what made him misbehave. Life without God could not be "good and right and true," and there was no way to figure how it could be until he came to the faith. When he came to the faith, he said he did not have to lose IQ points, but he could discern life entirely differently. That is the gift of faith. As the children of the light we can live in the light to see things in a different way from the manner in which the world perceives itself and its problems. We do not have to go into isolation, into a convent, or a monastery to get away from the world. We do not have to ignore the world. We have the freedom to live within the world and yet not become a part of it. We can see and behold the world as God's rule and realm. We can see the creation as God's gift to us. We can see the communities where we work and live as places where we can work for what is "good and right and true" for the benefit of others. To live as the children of light is to see all of life through the spectacles of the faith.

Find What Is Pleasing

Paul writes that the fruit of the light is "found in all that is good and right and true." Philosophers through the ages have searched for the ultimates of truth and beauty. Jaroslav Pelikan wrote *Fools For Christ,* a book in which he examined the thought of Christian philosophers. He noted the pitfall of all great thinkers is to personify what is good and right and true and make idols of them. Paul indicates we should escape the pitfall of such idolatry by making our Lord the center of our thought. He writes, "Try to find out what is pleasing to the Lord." We do not have to be great philosophers to recognize how readily people can make their favorite opinions into absolutes and worship them. We catch that as we hear the extremists who tend to radicalize issues. Paul would have us recognize how ambiguous much of life is. We experience ambiguity when we try to help someone only to discover that we

44

hurt someone else in the process. There are all kinds of homely slogans by which people deal with ambiguities. People will say they rob Peter to pay Paul. Or they excuse their own ambivalence by saying that there are two sides to everything.

However, Paul would have us know that we have to take seriously the business of working for what is good and right and true. We will have to work prayerfully at doing what is "pleasing to the Lord." *Epiphany* is one of a trilogy of novels by Ferral Sams, a physician who is also a novelist. The story is about Gregry McHune, a blue collar worker, who is socially inept and the victim of serious injustices. Slowly he develops a deep relationship with his physician Mark Goddard. He learns to trust Goddard and the doctor's explanation about the kingdom of heaven within you. Eventually he confesses to a plot that would involve a serious crime and then avoids it, but knows he must leave town for his own safety. The doctor asks him during their farewell what inhibited him from the act of violence. He replies he realized the business of the kingdom of heaven within you and that Jesus did his dead-level best to teach us the good way to live. As Paul would say, Gregry worked at finding out what is pleasing to the Lord. We must do so also, because our Lord did his dead-level best on the cross to make that possible for all of us.

Avoid Works Of Darkness

Paul would add that the children of light are not completely out of the woods as far as danger is concerned. The world and works of darkness are all around us. He writes, "Take no part in the unfruitful works of darkness, but instead expose them." The works of darkness do not always appear as darkness. They may appear shiny, bright, attractive, and comforting. All one has to do is recognize that when one listens to a half hour broadcast of the news, we hear half of that air time used to bombard us with the latest attractions we should definitely have to buy to be happy. Paul also mentions the shameful things people do secretly. Some scholars believe he was referring to secret cults and religions that performed all kind of shameful acts. That may be, but Paul could include the host of things people perpetrate in secret. The secret sins could be sexual licentiousness, embezzlement, robbery, and the like.

Police will tell you to protect your home you should have your house well lit, because the shameful people who are robbers and looters like to work in the dark. They hate the light. Yet people may be prone to the works of darkness because of their pitiful inability to shake the darkness. In Patricia Cornwell's novel, *Point Of Origin,* Peter Marino, captain of the Richmond Police Department, acknowledges his lack of proper care for his person. He is an example of the drunkenness and debauchery of which Paul warns in our text. Marino confesses to his poor health nourished by his smoking, drinking, and poor eating habits. He thinks of himself as an old slob, biting a poison cookie each day along with his steak, biscuits, beer, and whiskey. What Marino adds is that there is no reason for him to change. He sees the darkness as a wall in front of him, and, the worst is, that there is nothing behind the wall for him.

Wake Up!

In contrast to a world which is content to live in the darkness, relishes the darkness, or is the victim of the darkness, Paul challenges us not only to live in the light but to expose everything to the light. Quoting from what may have been an early Christian hymn based on a passage in Isaiah (60:1), Paul writes, "Sleeper, awake! Rise from the dead, and Christ will shine on you." Surrounded by a world of darkness, it is easy for us to be lulled asleep also and to ignore the dangers around us. It is especially true for us who live in a nation of luxury and prosperity. It is a comfortable world in which our scientific advances and creations have given us enormous advantages to make us comfortable.

Daniel Boorstin wrote an excellent book about the remarkable human capacity for invention and creation. The book is titled *The Creators: A History Of Heroes Of The Imagination.* Boorstin quotes one observer of humanity's achievements. The writer was overawed by the successes in the creation of so many arts and sciences. He mentions architecture, clothing, husbandry, transportation, sculpture, and painting. He cites the millions of inventions against others in terms of arms, poisons, engines, and stratagems. Part of the human defenses are the thousands of medicines and the various food creations. That is in brief what Boorstin was quoting from Saint Augustine writing in the fifth century. Imagine what Saint Augustine would write about the achievements in our generation! Yet Augustine noted that in spite of all these remarkable creations, there was no proper measure of the advance of humankind. And there is no sign of endless progress on earth. Of all that has been invented and created, all achievements point to our mortality with no clue as to how we come to eternal life. That is why the Apostle Paul, four centuries earlier, and for that matter in our day, can say, "Sleeper, awake! Rise from the dead, and Christ will shine on you."

Live In The Light

To live in the light is not only to live with the understanding of who we are and what we should be doing here. To live in the light is to live with the high certainty and absolute assurance that we are the children of God slated for eternity. The Christ who shines on us is the One who points the way in life, and he also points the way to eternity. That way is a path our Lord himself blazed by his life, suffering, death, resurrection, and ascension to return to the Father.

Come what may, no matter how often we suffer depression, feel like misfits, feel anxiety about the creation, or feel as though life has no purpose, we can be aroused from those dark thoughts, feelings, and sensations to move once again into the light, because the Risen and glorified Christ is at our sides to take us by the hand and lead us through the maze of darkness into the light of grace, love, forgiveness, and hopefulness. It is in the Living Christ that we can see and understand life, as opposed to being in the dark. It is also in the Christ that we can live as children of the light, that is, we can strive to find out and to do what is pleasing to the Lord. That is the experience the Apostle wants to make common for us as members of the body of Christ. In the beginning we noted the Apostle had reminded us we all have once been children of darkness, and it is true we can still be threatened by the darkness. However, now in Christ we can live together and work together in the blessings of the light which the Christ shines upon us.

A Higher Lifestyle

A gripping and extremely well told story of how the law works out in the lives of people is *Midwives*, a novel by Chris Bohjalian. The principal character in the story is Sibyl Danforth, an unlicensed Vermont midwife. Isolated and trapped by an unwelcome ice storm, Sibyl is not able to reach the hospital with a patient having great difficulty during her labor. Sibyl performs a cesarean section on the patient when she believes the mother has died of a stroke in trying to give birth to her child. Sibyl does save the child, but she immediately becomes the subject of investigation by the law for liability malpractice and more. The account of that investigation, which results in a trial, gives us insight into the nature of the law.

The law is persistent, fastidious, and tenacious. The law is demanding and protective. The law produces guilt. The novel helps us to recognize how helpless one is before the law, as the law works through its accusatory role. *Midwives* is not simply about the debate over the practice of the legality of licensed or non-licensed midwives. It is an excellent case history about law. If you can gain some insight into the nature of the law from such a story, then you can deepen your understanding of how the Apostle Paul realistically assesses the function of law in our lives and makes an appeal for a lifestyle higher than one lived under the law. That is the subject of the Second Reading appointed for today.

The Struggle With The Law
One must understand at the very beginning that the Apostle Paul is not opposed to the law. Very often people who want to

stress the importance of love and freedom are opposed to the law. They are called "antinomians." That means, they resist the functions of the νομοσ, the Greek word for "law." That can take many different forms of resistance. In counseling, some therapists may make the client feel as though there is no reason for feeling guilt. There are times when people do have a false sense of guilt. However, most of the time people feel guilt because they are guilty under the law and recognize their guilt. However, some people identify themselves as libertarians. People who make libertarianism a political stance want government to function as little as possible on the basis of law.

Socially people may be libertarian to the extent they feel they should be able to live in total freedom. The sexual revolution that began in the sixties in this country is one form of that kind of antinomianism. There are people who organize themselves against the law. We think of the communes of the sixties and seventies that attempted to develop ideal forms of communal living without the benefit of the law. A recent novel by Ken Follett titled *The Hammer Of Eden* treats the matter of antinomianism. Members of a commune, called the Hammer of Eden, threaten to cause earthquakes to make the Governor of California refrain from destroying their valley by creating a dam as a source of power. The leader of the commune meditates on five maxims of the commune: Meditation is life, Money makes one poor; Marriage is the greatest infidelity; When no one owns anything, all own everything; Do what you like is the only law. That is organized antinomianism. Generally, the most common form of antinomianism is the final maxim of the commune, "Do what you like is the only law." We are all guilty of that, and we do struggle with the law every day.

A Legalistic Society

Our struggle with the law is intensified by the fact that we live in a legalistic society. The laws begin at home with the do's and don'ts parents must establish for their children. Children who fail to learn discipline at home will have difficulty with discipline at school, at work, and within the community. It is no secret that a major problem in our society today is that too many parents have not disciplined their children and are in reality afraid of their children. Our national debates also focus on the fact that we must reestablish authority within the schools so that there can be more discipline within the classrooms, beginning with dress codes, and the like. We have complicated the problems of discipline within the homes and school by making laws about discipline that is regarded as child abuse. In the work place and in the community, relations between peoples are also regulated more and more by laws. Union and management have made their own laws. Now much of that is also governed by state and national laws.

The unprecedented growth of our technology and media of communication call for constant vigilance and observation for the manner in which the growth of problems in these areas can be regulated by law. Our national debates about laws and regulations are also intensified by the increases in our population. It is a matter of more human behavior having to be controlled in more densely populated areas. Then, of course, we find our national debates focusing more and more on ethical issues like drug abuse, abortion, bearing of arms, and racism. At every turn we take, new laws and regulations have to be made. Of necessity we must live within a legal community.

The Flesh Is The Problem

The Apostle Paul recognized that the law has to perform this kind of function in the world. God is very much involved in this business of regulating human behavior in the creation. God is in charge of it all. Luther would call it God's Kingdom of the Left Hand in which God rules with the stuff of the law. The Law is God's wrath at work in the world. God wants to push down on the world to make the world behave. However, Paul also saw that as God pushes and pulls on people with the law to make them sweat, people ought to look up to get some help from God. In this endless struggle with the law, we ought to recognize where the problem lies. In the previous chapter, Paul placed the blame where it belongs. The fact that things are still unruly in the world is because people are what they are. It is not the weakness or the fault of the law. The faultiness is within us.

Every one of the Ten Commandments and every law no matter how small or large promises that if we love our neighbors as ourselves, everything will be okay. Yet it isn't, because we struggle with our own sinful selfish flesh. The law, Paul says, promises life, but because we do not keep it, the law punishes us with death. The National Rifle Association has it right. It isn't that guns are bad. The bad people abuse the use of guns. But if we follow that argument, we have to get rid of everybody, because all people are bad. It is within ourselves that the real struggle with the law goes on, because we have a struggle within our own flesh. The law says one thing, but our selfish flesh wants to do something else. The law, Paul says, is spiritual. It is holy. However, it is weakened by our flesh that wants things its own way. Paul says it is as though we are enslaved to our own flesh and to sin. We know better, but we find ourselves choosing do to the wrong or the forbidden thing. What we need is to find a way of responding to what our mind says rather than obey what our flesh says. Paul had a way of talking about our weaknesses as a catering to the flesh. When Paul speaks about the flesh, he is not writing about flesh as in flesh and bones. Rather Paul means the total person opposed to God.

Stuck With The Flesh

Paul sees that the problem about the flesh, a life lived apart from God's Spirit, is compounded by the fact that the flesh is stuck on or with the flesh. Paul writes, "Those who live according to the flesh set their minds on the things of the flesh." We cannot expect otherwise. Jesus talked about the unproductive vine (John 15), and Luther noted that a bad tree brings forth bad fruit. The problem is not a minor flaw. The nature of the flesh is that it is a defect that contaminates the whole being. The total being is preoccupied with the things of the flesh. Some rich insights into just how perversely the flesh is oriented to the flesh can be found in *Tuesdays With Morrie*. The book is a record of conversations between Mitch Albon and Morrie Schwartz. Morrie is a professor of sociology dying from Lou Gehrig's disease. Mitch Albon is a sports writer for the Detroit *Free Press* and one of Morrie's former students.

When Albon learns of Morrie's illness, he makes it a point to fly to Morrie's home each Tuesday morning for a dialogue with him about his illness and impending death. Morrie observes how differently people would live if they knew they were dying. People could forego many pleasures, the pursuits of their greed, their need to amass material things, and they could concentrate on loving others. However, he noted that all people know they are going to die. The problem is they do not believe it! That reveals how badly people are hooked on their own flesh. The one thing that is the most certain in their lives, and they know it to be so, is death. Yet somehow they are so preoccupied with the flesh they do not believe in the reality and the consequences of their own death.

The Flesh Is Hostile To God

Because people are so preoccupied with the preservation of their own flesh, it is understandable they would like to think as little as possible about death as the worst that happens to them. Who wants to think about death? Yet the greater problem is that the preoccupation people have with their flesh makes them hostile to God. Paul explains that the problem is that people should know they are not just putting off the question of death. They are putting off God. God is the One who gives life. God is the One who also takes life. People have invented their own platitudes about death. Even Morrie, the sociology professor at Brandeis, could say while he was dying that the only life worth living is the one worth dying. Existentialist philosophers have surmised the only legitimate question to contemplate is the question of death. Yet that is wrong, and far from what is absolutely basic, which is, to think about God. That is why Paul says people who set their minds only on the flesh are hostile to God.

People refuse to submit to God's law, which ends in death to those who do not love God. Paul says it is so bad that they cannot think properly about God. The flesh is so warped that they cannot submit to God's law. Paul writes, "The mind that is set on the flesh ... does not submit to God's law — indeed it cannot, and those who are in the flesh cannot please God." What Paul is explaining to us helps us to understand why things in the world are as they are. Judged from the side of God's law, the world is all upside down. The cultures of the world run counter to the will of God and have always done so. Left to their own resources, people do not make their way back to God on their own. However, it does not have to be that way. Paul's reason for stating the reality of the human condition is to point out the fact that God does give a way out of the human predicament by sending to people the gift of the Spirit. Paul's appeal to us is that we accept the higher lifestyle possible for us because of the presence of God's Spirit.

You Are In The Spirit

In spite of a realistic and hopeless view of life lived under the influence of the flesh, or the mind hostile and helpless before God, Paul reminds us we live on an entirely different plane. Paul writes, "You are not in the flesh; you are in the Spirit, since the Spirit of God dwells in you." He goes on to explain that because the Spirit of God lives within us, the body has already been put to death because of sin. We have to understand that correctly. Some older people are likely to think they understand that well, because there are days when one can wake up in the morning feeling like death warmed over. Paul does not mean that. He means that our lives no longer have to be controlled only by what the body or flesh dictate. The flesh does not have to have control of us. In the Spirit, we are alive to righteousness, not to sin.

We seek to do that which conforms to the will of God, not simply to our own selfish dictates or what other people who live after the flesh dictate. That begins with young children. They not only learn how to obey the will of God by being obedient to parents, but they learn how to say, "No," to the temptations of playmates. Later on they are equipped by the Spirit to say, "No," to the temptations of the teen years, to drugs and to all the lures that are present in growing to adulthood. Life in the Spirit continues this struggle against the flesh through all the periods and ages of one's life until one comes to the end of life in this world. One experiences this sensitivity to the struggle the life of the Spirit has over the life of the flesh sometimes with pain and heartache. However, one also has the rewards of joy and pleasure in a life that is able to

54

act without the pressure of the law or the pressure of peers and the world. It becomes a higher lifestyle, because it is life from above.

You Are Alive To God

There is a popular Hebrew book called *The Hesed Boomerang*. The message of the book explains the rewards and blessings of living under divine mercy. The business of living by the Spirit of God is not to be a spoilsport and to live under wet blankets. The life of the spirit is filled with joys, laughter, and confidence. The reason for this is the Spirit of God who dwells in us. Paul says, "The Spirit of him who raised Christ from the dead will give life to your mortal bodies also through his spirit that dwells in you." The life, the passion, the death, the resurrection, and the ascension of our Lord Jesus Christ give life to us. We do not have to say only that our Lord Jesus Christ died and rose again for us. The effects of his death and resurrection are within us. They have achieved a death within us. We are dead to sin means that sin does not control or condemn our lives.

That the Risen Christ lives in us means we are alive to God. We live to God by the manner in which our lives are directed to serve God by serving and living in others by love and grace. One does not have to read far to discover many writers and observers of human nature who believe that the crises of our age are disconnection and discontinuity. People sense this on all levels of relationships. However, they discover it also within themselves. We see the problem as the disconnection that people have from God. For us who know God's grace, love, mercy, and forgiveness in our Christ, we need not suffer such disconnection and discontinuity. By the faith through the gift of God's Spirit, we achieve wholeness with our God and with all eternity. This truly is a higher lifestyle. We do not have our heads in the clouds, but the Spirit from on high lives within us. This lifestyle in the Spirit of God is not a hands-off every day affair or reserved only for high holy days or Sundays. This is the application of the Spirit of God to the common, the nitty gritty, and the ordinary. We are not living high off the hog. We are living high off the Spirit.

A Meeting Of The Minds

ABC produced a television program titled *Strange World*. The story line of a rather dull episode was that a young scientist set out to transfer the memory of the mind from one person to another. The experiment was extended to transfer the experience of death in the mind of one person to another. In order to carry out his experiment the scientist decided to kill in order to transfer the brain fluids from the dead person to the live person. What triggered the experiment in the first place was a fascination with death. People are likely to believe that if somehow they are able to enter into the death experience, they will have some mastery over death. That notion is borne out by the flurry of publications which appeared for a time reporting near-death experiences. The trend was to try to find some commonality in what people experienced as they may have had their brush with death on the operating table or in some physical crisis in which they may have been dead for a very brief time.

As we begin this week of concentration on the passion and death of our Lord Jesus Christ, we are very much concerned with the matter of the death of our Lord and how it factors in our lives. With the lessons appointed for this day we anticipate the remembrance of the death of Jesus Christ as we meditate upon it in this Holy Week. However, what is obvious from the Second Reading from the Epistle of Paul the Apostle to the Philippians is that Paul is able to put a unique spin on the manner in which he deals with the subject of the death of Jesus.

Obedient To Death

What is unusual about the way Paul speaks about the death of our Lord is that he says we should have the "same mind" as Christ who became "obedient to the point of death." You are apt to retort that there is nothing remarkable about that. We all have to be obedient to death. There is no escaping death. That is even true of the person who commits suicide. The suicide becomes obedient to death, even though suicide seems a friendly exit from a dreadful form of living. What is different about the death of our Lord is that the path to our Lord's death was traveled a different way. Death interrupts our lives. It always seems to come at the wrong time. Sometimes it appears to come far too early. Other times death appears too late. We do not set the alarm for death to arrive at our fixed time. What Paul wants us to understand about how our Lord met his death is that Jesus literally went out to meet his death with a holy purpose and goal.

The Lord Jesus did not try to identify with death for the sole purpose of letting us know that he had done so in sympathy for us. The strategy was that the Son of the Father in heaven was sent into the world to take on death as the enemy. Death followed upon sin. Death was the judgment for failure to trust God. Death stood as a wall between God and humanity. The divine intention, then, was to focus on the means of dealing with death with a finality that would rob death completely of any rights to intimidate or judge people. The goal was not to minimize or assuage the pain that death brings, though those would be the fruits of dealing a knock-out blow to death. All of this implied that the strategy was not to view death as a physical problem or the end of physical life. Clearly the intention from the beginning was to recognize that death has to do with life as lived in trust of God or the failure to trust God as the Creator of life. Because life has its origin in God and is sustained by God, in order to deal with death one has to face the fact that one has to begin with one's attitude toward God. That is where the story of Jesus of Nazareth begins. That is how Paul understood it.

God's Equal

In order to help us appreciate what Jesus accomplished by going out to meet death, Paul quotes an early Christian hymn which is our reading for today. The hymn recalls that Jesus came into the world in the same condition as Adam. When God created the First Adam, God made a special feature of humanity's createdness. The first creatures were to stand in relationship to God. God gave to them of God's own Spirit. Consequently, the first creature could be called the "Son of God" (Luke 3:23). Likewise when Jesus was born into the world, he was born to the same advantage as Adam. Jesus could be called the Second Adam. The hymn says, "He was in the form of God." As the First Adam, Jesus was a person of the flesh, human in every way, from head to toe. However, Jesus, like the First Adam, was filled with the Spirit of God. But, the hymn goes on to say that Jesus "did not regard equality with God as something to be exploited." That was different from the First Adam.

We recall that the temptation in the garden was for the creatures to believe that they could be as God if they ate of the forbidden fruit. They wanted to exploit the business of being equal with God. They were already as God, but they doubted that they were, because the Tempter said they could be like God. They doubted what God had done for them was enough. They exploited the notion that they could be something more than they were to be "as God." That was the most ungodly thing they could have done. It was rank blasphemy. It was unbelief, the source of all sin, the same original sin we all engage in. Jesus avoided it. Jesus did not capitulate. Jesus did not "regard equality with God as something to be exploited."

In Human Form

Jesus did just the opposite from exploiting the equality with God. Jesus chose to be identified with us "in human form." The Creator became the creature. The reason Jesus chose to do so was to be able to roll back humanity to the innocence at the time of creation. In order to do so, Jesus had to take his place with us in the human order of things as they are now. Richard Fortey, an English paleontologist, has compiled the story of the development of the creation as we know it in a study titled *Life*. This study is a compilation from the date derived from the multitudinous evidences of the fossils of millions of years ago. The generous deposits of traces of the development of life stretched over eons of time tell the story of how life emerged on the remarkable planet earth that we call home. Mr. Fortey sticks to the hard evidence of what has been distributed as a remarkable account of how life has emerged.

The paleontologist sticks to the facts as they have been discovered. There is no intention to explain more than what has been found. No meaning is applied to the life which has emerged. No philosophy or theology interprets the material. But there is one observation of fact that cannot be denied. The human that evolved from this trail of life is, Fortey notes, the only animal that has deceived itself. To be sure, there is abundant evidence of that. That is the telltale evidence of the human condition. We suffer from the fact that human behavior belies the wonder, the mystique, the marvel, the profundity, the beauty, and the majesty of life. The psalmist can extol in hymnic phrases that we are fearfully and wondrously made, but in the next breath bemoan that we must cry from the depths of woe of our sin and unbelief. As humans we have blown it. We have messed up the gift of life God has given us. That is why our Lord Jesus Christ came to be among us in human form. Christ came to reverse the process of devolution that we have introduced into the creation.

A Death On The Cross

The reversal that Jesus could bring to life for us could take place only through his dying. Theologians of other ages have wondered if it was truly necessary for Jesus to have died. Some have suggested that simply the incarnation, the birth of the Christ as human, could be counted redemptive enough. That would be to say, innocence was restored to humanity through the One who graced our world with his human presence. Some suggested that the blood shed at the circumcision of our Lord was enough blood shed for the atonement for the world. There are always those who say the value of the life of Jesus of Nazareth was that he was a model of how life should be lived and can be lived. That should be enough for us. Some say you don't even have to think of him as the Son of God to believe that. None of that comes close to understanding how Jesus "humbled himself and became obedient to the point of death — even death on the cross."

It was in the acts of moving to the cross willfully, pointedly, and dramatically that Jesus struggled with what plagued the human condition. It was disobedience to the Creator, unbelief before God, the failure to rely on God's goodness that had brought death to the world, because life without God is death. Jesus had to believe God in the face of that intrusion into life we know as death. Jesus submitted to God in obedience and faith by yielding to death on the cross. The older eucharistic liturgy reminds us that by a tree he overcame him who once overcame us by a tree. At the tree of the cross, Jesus redeemed what went wrong at the tree in the Garden of Eden. For us that means that our Lord Jesus Christ endured this death on the cross to reverse the judgment that falls around our ears in death.

He Is Exalted

It is because Jesus of Nazareth died the death that he did, we can now face death ourselves with the conviction that we can also face death not as judgment but as the step into eternity with God. Jesus removed the sting and the power of death, because he faced it under the judgment that should befall us. That is, Jesus died as the worst sinner of all, one judged as a blasphemer of God and an insurrectionist against the government. These sins were the worst crimes against both God and the state. He thereby represented the most heinous crimes of all of humankind. He died a death for us all under the worst kind of convictions we could have suffered. Yet he did so believing that God would still count him innocent.

God judged Jesus a sinner by the law that condemned him. But God judged him innocent by the faith that he still trusted the Father would raise him from the dead. And God did raise him from the dead. Thereby God exalted Jesus "and gave him the name above every name, so that at the name of Jesus every knee should bend." Jesus proved God is faithful. God can be believed to deliver us from the worst of conditions and situations — death itself. Jesus proved that it is done by faith. Jesus became the source and the goal of faith at the same time. That is why every knee should bend before him. Mozart's *Requiem*, regarded as a masterpiece, was not completed by Mozart actually before his untimely death. There are those who suggest he wrote it for himself, though he had been commissioned for its composition. If he did write it with his own situation in mind, it is the outpouring of deep faith. "King of majesty tremendous, / Who dost free salvation send us, / Fount of pity then befriend us." Literally in the Latin, "Who saving saves free." You know the Latin for "free," that is, *gratis*. We all can appeal to him for salvation. It is difficult to imagine Mozart did not believe what was written here. The music says he did. And so should we. Paul's hymn says, "At the name of Jesus every knee should bend."

Every Tongue Confess

At the "name of Jesus every knee should bend" expresses how as the redeemed people of God we should bow in repentance, humility, and adoration to the One who is our Savior. Paul predicts eventually every knee "in heaven and on earth and under the earth" should have to give homage to the One who has been exalted by God. Paul adds, "And every tongue should confess that Jesus Christ is Lord to the glory of God the Father." Jesus warned that at his great day, however, not everyone who calls his name or says, "Lord, Lord," will enter the kingdom. The words of Paul imply that we cannot give lip service to this Jesus with simple formulas. To "confess with the tongue" implies that the confession on the tongue and lips must be the confession of commitment in the heart.

The late Robert Shaw liked to tell of an experience he had in leading a workshop of music teachers and choir directors one summer in New York City. At the close of the workshop, the participants were privileged to give a concert of sacred songs in Carnegie Hall. The songs were picked from favorites they had sung or directed in their church choirs. Just before the concert he could tell how nervous the choir was about singing in a hall famed for the parade of great stars and renowned choirs which had performed there. He told his choir they had nothing to fear. He said they brought to the hall a spirit and faith that was rare among most of the performances, which had been solely professional. Mr. Shaw commented that the concert of his workshop choir was absolutely stellar that evening, because his choir members had furnished the inspiration for singing favorite choral numbers they sang mostly in their church choirs back home. That was truly confessing with the tongue the faith that lives in the heart.

Christ Is Lord

What we confess with the tongue about Jesus, Paul says, is "that Jesus Christ is Lord, to the glory of God the Father." Curiously, the Matthaen account of our Lord's Passion records that those who confessed that Jesus was Lord at the crucifixion did not come from the ranks of his followers. It was Pilate who paid tribute to him with the superscription on the cross which read, "This is Jesus King of the Jews." It was a Roman centurion at the foot of the cross who confessed, "Truly this was the Son of God." It was Joseph of Arimathea, not identified as a disciple, who boldly came forward to ask Pilate for the body of Jesus in order to give the Savior a decent burial. The other evangelists indicate that one of the malefactors, crucified along with Jesus, gave testimony of his faith in Jesus as the King who could give him entrance into our Lord's kingdom.

How fortunate the recorded story was not about timid disciples, who suddenly became inspired and heroic in confessing profound faith in Jesus at the cross. Rather the confessions come from hardened hearts which had been moved to recognize already at the cross the hour our Lord called his "hour of glory," the Father exalted the Son so hearts could be moved to faith. That is a blessing for us. We know none of us, sinners that we are, need be excluded from the death benefits of our Lord. The confession of the dying thief gives us greatest assurance. That confession was the inspiration for the last lines of Bernard of Clairvaux's hymn, "O Sacred Head, Now Wounded." The lines are "Remind me of your Passion / When my last hour draws nigh. / These eyes, new faith receiving, / From you shall never move; / For he who dies believing / Dies safely in your love." The last line is that to have the mind of Christ, as Paul explains, is to know that both in life and death we can live in the faith. Because of our Lord Jesus Christ, we can be obedient to God not only in life but in death itself.

Maundy Thursday
1 Corinthians 11:23-26

All Baked Into One Loaf

On Passion Sunday we took note of the work of Richard Fortey, an English paleontologist, who published a book called *Life*. The work is a popular summary of all the evidences of the wide distribution of fossils that inform us as to how life began on this amazing planet of ours. What is still missing for paleontologists and anthropologists as well, are fossil remains of someone who can be recognized as the predecessor of human beings we know as *homo sapiens*. What is clear, however, is that civilization had its roots in those areas where grain was first domesticated. The grinding of grain and the preparation of bread is the first act of civilization. Anthropologists have known that for some time. What is intriguing for us is that civilization did take place in the area between the Tigris and the Euphrates some ten thousand years ago.

Fortey takes note of the fact that in the scriptures the breaking and sharing of bread are often the simplest and most profound expressions of caring and fellowship. The breaking of bread is social. The breaking of bread does create community and society. In confirmation and first communion classes we can explain to young people how a host or hostess can make them feel much more comfortable in an adult gathering where they are bored. When the host or the hostess invites them to table to share cake and ice cream, children can be made to feel they are accepted and feel a part of the group. Meals do the same for adults. However, on this Maundy Thursday we speak of a meal our Lord instituted which has even greater social and communal significance.

The Eucharist Is Social

The Second Reading appointed for Maundy Thursday is from a letter of the Apostle Paul to the Church at Corinth. The context for Paul's inclusion of the words of institution of the Lord's supper which Paul had received from the Twelve was that the Apostle was remonstrating with the behavior of some of the people at the celebration of the Lord's Supper. It was custom at Corinth at the communion celebration to have a love feast before the service. It was something like our church dinners. However, these people brought their own meals. Some of them overdid it with their eating and drinking and ignored the poor people who had little or nothing. Some of them drank too much and got drunk. Paul wanted the Corinthians to know such behavior at the meal was not acceptable. This was not the social kind of eating and drinking to be associated with the Lord's Supper. In fact, it achieved the opposite effect. Such eating and drinking was not social in creating community but divisive.

Paul recites the words of institution to make clear what was intended in the communal meal of the Lord's Supper. On the basis of the eucharistic formula, we call the meal a "communion." That Latin word means "one with." In the communion we are made one with our Lord Jesus Christ. We are being made one with our God. However, we are also being made one with one another. We become community in the very act of this eating and supping with one another. Luther says in the Lord's Supper God bakes us all into one loaf. As we all eat of the bread we all become one in Christ. This creates intimacy for us not only with God but with one another. Young are united with the old, the rich with the poor, the black with the white, the men with women. Thus it is a special eating and drinking. To be sure, people can make the dinner table something other than that. The meal can become a sign of elitism and snobbery or it can end in heated argument that divides. Our Lord's Supper was instituted to create the best and most intimate of unions between God and people, and people and people.

The Eucharist Is Remembrance

As we gather together at the table our Lord Jesus Christ has set for us to experience union with him and one another, we do not set our own agenda for the table talk. Our Lord has provided for that in a special way. When Jesus instituted this special meal for us, he said that we are to do this eating and drinking in remembrance of him. What Jesus means by remembrance is the Hebrew understanding of remembrance, that is, to repeat something as though it were happening for the first time. Plimouth Colony is recreated in Massachusetts where the Pilgrims first landed in 1620. Those working in the colony speak and act as though they were the first residents who came to live in that colony. There are other such historic sites where the people running the historic establishments act as the first residents in order to have the visitors experience firsthand what had taken place there. As we attend the Lord's Supper, we are to experience this meal as though our Lord himself were feeding us in the Upper Room with the disciples. It was for this reason that the Church developed a liturgical calendar, in which we rehearse different events in the life of our Lord. We remember, in an original sense, the incidents from his life, from his birth at Bethlehem to his death, resurrection, and ascension. As we hear anew how the life of our Lord unfolds from his birth, his ministry, suffering, death, resurrection, and ascension, we are caught up in those life experiences to make what our Lord accomplished through his life, death, and resurrection our own. That is why we introduce different rites and colors to accompany the reading of the word to set the stage for such remembrance.

The Eucharist Is Forgiveness

The benefits of the celebration of the Lord's Supper are all related to what God accomplished for us though God's Son. In the words of institution Paul sets forth, Jesus says plainly that the bread is his body given for us. The cup, Jesus says, is the new covenant in his blood. This is the language of sacrifice and the promise God attached to the sacrifice. God had established a covenant with ancient Israel. The covenant was to make clear God would be the God of the people and they would be his people. In order for that to be made clear as possible for the people, God instituted a system in which animals would be sacrificed as offerings for the sins of the people, so that they would be acceptable before God. They did not have to do anything. The priest made the sacrifice so the people could see God's love and forgiveness in action for them.

Now Jesus was to be both the priest and the sacrifice to guarantee forgiveness for the people. It is the same God who acts in the same gracious and forgiving way. What is different is that before, the sacrificial system was the sign to the people of God's gracious and forgiving attitude toward Israel. Now Jesus is that sign for us. To know that is what is being signaled to us in the Lord's Supper is to receive much blessing. Luther would say the words "given and shed for you" are assurances to us that we receive from our Lord's gracious hand and heart the "forgiveness of sins, life, and salvation, for where there is forgiveness of sins there is also life and salvation." The forgiveness of sins clears away all that would stand between God and us, between us and God. That also implies we know when we come to the Lord's Supper it is because we are in dire need of the forgiveness of sins. We are all sinners and most helpless in trying to find our way out of guilt and the consequences our guilt has earned for us. The observance of the Lord's Supper, then, provides that kind of confrontation with our God that brings us to our knees recognizing what sinners we are but then confronting the God who sets aside judgment on the sinner to offer the gift of forgiveness and eternal life.

The Eucharist Is Presence

God furnishes this experience of the special meal as a confrontation with God to enable us to focus on the relationship God creates with us. God wants to make it easy for us. God addresses our need to have some signs to signal what God wants to communicate is for real. Our age has known the remarkable advantage of the telephone for communicating, be it business or personal matters. Now we add the blessings of fax machines, E-mail, and the Internet. Radio and television have extended our ability to be a part of scenes in every area of the world. We are able to communicate and to receive personal communications universally. The Eucharist is the means by which our Lord communicates himself to us in a unique way. Paul reports that when Jesus broke the bread and gave it to his disciples he said, "This is my body that is for you." When he shared the cup with the disciples he said, "This cup is the new covenant in my blood."

Because Jesus acted and spoke as he did, we call this action the communication of his Real Presence. By this we say, Christ is really and truly present in the Lord's Supper. There have been all kinds of efforts to explain how Christ is present in the sacred meal. Some have said Jesus is only symbolically present, spiritually present, or that the bread and wine are changed into his body and blood. We do not know the "how" of it. We preserve the mystery by believing in his presence, because he promises to be present. To make the point in teaching about communion in confirmation and first communion classes, one can use the illustration of television. Ask the children if they know how television works. Some one is sure to answer, "You turn it on." Right. Even though most of us cannot explain how television works, we turn it on. In the Lord's Supper we "turn it on" by faith trusting in our Lord's promise to be present in the eating and drinking.

The Eucharist Is Representation

Because we believe Christ is truly present in the Lord's Supper, the Apostle says, "As often as you eat this bread and drink this cup, you proclaim the Lord's death." There was a time when Christians debated whether Paul's statement implied Jesus was sacrificed anew each time the Lord's Supper was celebrated. If so, that would imply the celebrant would have the power to make Christ a sacrifice each time. To be sure, Christ is not re-presented in the sacrament. Yet he is represented in the sacramental action as the communicants proclaim his death. Each observance of the sacrament is a statement to the world that we believe in this Lord Jesus Christ, who died for us.

Gordon Lathrop has published a liturgical theology called *Holy Things*. A major contribution Lathrop makes is to help us to learn the proper understanding of the word *sacrifice* when speaking of our Lord. Actually, Lathrop says, it is the wrong word for us. Citing Justin, one of the early fathers, Lathrop pointed out that our God does not need ritualistic killing to be appeased. Furthermore, Jesus was not sacrificed. Jesus was executed. So when we speak of the Lord's Supper we should not be thinking of Jesus being sacrificed anew. Rather we should recognize, as Paul says, that we proclaim the Lord's death. With that emphasis we should note that we are representing again to the world the story of the One who came to live and die for us that we might know the grace, mercy, and forgiveness of God. Our celebration of the Lord's Supper is a statement of faith, trust, and thanksgiving by which we are marked as the people of God who are willing to serve in the name of our Lord Jesus Christ. The gifts of God for the people of God are the Word and the sacraments which are ours to celebrate in thanksgiving. To use the Greek word for thanksgiving, *eucharist*, we are a eucharistic people, a thankful and thanksgiving people.

The Eucharist Is Anticipation

As the people of God who give witness to and offer thanksgiving for our Lord Jesus Christ in the celebration of the Eucharist we also indicate our anticipation of his Coming Again. We are not only a thankful people but we are also a hopeful people. The whole sacramental action from beginning to end is premised on the promise that our Lord Jesus Christ gave to his disciples when he instituted the Supper for them. Jesus celebrated a seder meal and his new Supper with them. Jesus promised he would not celebrate the meal with them in this personal way until he celebrated the meal in his Father's kingdom (Matthew 14:25). After Jesus rose from the dead, the Gospels record that he appeared to his followers a liberal number of times. On some of those occasions we read that he broke bread with them. The description of those events employ the eucharistic language suggesting that he celebrated the meal with them. This was a way of saying that the age of the Kingdom of God had dawned with the resurrection of our Lord.

Now we eat of the bread and drink of the cup in this sacramental meal in the sure hope that he will come again. We eat the meal in anticipation of the Risen Christ coming in all his glory that we might meet him. We meet him in the Sacrament in his Real Presence by the promise he has given us to be present. We anticipate his Coming Again by virtue of the promise that he also made to eat and drink with us in the Father's kingdom. Those promises are made sure, real, and certain by the death and resurrection of our Lord Jesus Christ. Our anticipation of his Coming is no wild dream. It is a sure and certain hope. Nothing else in all of your life is more sure and more certain than this, that the One who created and redeemed you will come again to take you to himself. You can eat this meal with that high hope.

The Eucharist Is For You

We cannot speak of the Supper our Lord instituted for us without recognizing how personal Jesus made the supper. As he distributed the elements in the Supper, Paul reports Jesus said, "This is my body that is for you." In the same way he said, "This cup is the new covenant in my blood. Do this as often as you drink it." It is for you. Luther could not say enough about the fact that it is "for you." The Christmas angel had announced, "Unto you is born in the city of David, a Savior who is Christ the Lord." He was born for you. He lived for you. He died for you. He arose for you. He will come again for you. Here is where God focuses on us. We think of how we should use the occasion of the sacrament to focus on the words and promises of God. We should remember this is the way God focuses on us.

God pinpoints the moment, the place, and the means in which he brings all the benefits of grace and love to bear on us. This is the meal on which to feed when we have self doubts, when we are loaded with guilt, when we are worried or fearsome of the future. This is the meal on which to feed when we have reason to express our thanks and love to God. This is the meal on which to feed when we feel lonely, cut off, or abandoned. This is the meal on which to feed when we feel we cannot believe or we need the faith to be restored and renewed. You name it. This meal is for you whether you are on a spiritual high or in the spiritual depths. So in whatever condition we find ourselves we can come in faith and rely on the Christ who is really present to make us whole. Like the centurion who sent for Jesus to heal his servant, as we come we can say, "Lord, I am not worthy that you should come under my roof, but speak the word only and your servant will be healed." By that we mean the roof of our heads, and we are the servants who will be healed by his presence for us in the sacrament.

Good Friday
Hebrews 10:16-25

The New And Living Way

The prominence of Good Friday has been lost on the world. School spring recess has popularized family excursions during holidays that were once regarded as holy days. The Christian Church has not been able to maintain the piety formerly obeyed quietly and strictly in the Holy Week of the Church's liturgical calendar. If we are nostalgic and saddened by the absence of worthy notable mournful Christian devotion, we can make up for it by serious concentration on the message of Good Friday. The Epistle to the Hebrews is especially helpful in that regard. Written in the last part of the first century, this highly polished Greek essay may have been intended for the sake of Jewish Christians who were thinking of returning to the practice of their Hebrew faith. Or it may have been aimed at Jews to demonstrate how the faith in our Lord Jesus Christ excelled but is in fulfillment of the Hebrew faith.

The writer may have been Apollos, the sophisticated Greek colleague of the Apostle Paul. Whoever he was, the writer clearly set out to show how the Person of our Lord Jesus Christ in whom God revealed love and grace was vastly superior to the many ways and many persons in whom God had given clear revelations of God's grace. Jesus, the Son of God, was superior to the angels. He was equally superior to Moses and Joshua, the great leaders of the Hebrew people, who helped them to be shaped as the people of God. Jesus was superior to the high priest and to the priestly system. The priestly system also produced the sacrificial system which was intended to show that the sacrifice was always a sign of God's grace. The sacrifices of animals were to assure the people God had made atonement for them to be God's people. Good Friday is an especially good time to concentrate on the sacrifice of Christ as pertinent for our sakes.

A New Approach

The writer to the Hebrews stresses the superiority of the sacrifice of Jesus on the cross over the former sacrificial system, because he wants to make a special point of the fact that God also thinks of it as improvement. The author quotes from the Prophet Jeremiah who writes of God's new covenant that will be a direct approach to the people. This was not only new for the people of God, but it is also different from what the world would expect of God. In *The Bible Makes Sense*, Walter Brueggemann, a Hebrew Testament scholar, writes of the odd perspective the Bible has of God. The Bible does not attempt to describe the fullness of God with the infinitude of God's characteristics. Rather the Bible insists that we get to know God by what God does.

Ordinarily people want to talk about God in terms of the magnitude of God's power. When the Bible talks about God's power it refers to what God does for us so that we do not have to fear God. Just so the Apostle Paul says that God's power was made perfect in weakness. Paul was referring to God's becoming weak at the cross so that God could die for us. The writer to the Hebrews takes the position that this was the fulfillment of the covenant, the manner in which God showed this was a once-for-all sacrifice that puts the matter of God's forgiveness right on our hearts and reveals to our minds what God is really like. That makes for a new approach. We no longer have to have someone make a sacrifice for us. We do not have to have someone make an approach to God for us. Rather, our writer says, "Therefore my friends ... we have confidence to enter the sanctuary by the new and living way he opened for us."

The New Covenant In Us

The certainty of our situation is emphasized by the writer in assuring us that what God did in fulfillment of the covenant in our Lord Jesus Christ is within us. We should not think of the covenant or the words of God as being outside of ourselves, that is, as

74

some laws or words out there waiting to be imposed on us. The nature of God's covenant with us is that it is the intimate expression of God's love for us. It is the same as when the words of the lover, "I love you," are no longer just words to try to win the heart of the dear one the lover pursues. It is when the words, "I love you," take root in the heart of the one pursued, and the one who is loved knows the words live in the heart to bind them together. People have different views of what a covenant relationship means.

In *Renewing the Covenant*, Dr. Leonora Leet noted that some can see the covenant in terms of obvious manifestations the Creation has made within the creation itself. Simply, as creatures we are dependent upon and bound to the Creator. Or the covenant can be renewed through the mosaic law with great emphasis upon the Sabbath which is designed to relate us to the Creator. Then there is a covenant of love that binds us in love and service to God. Still another way to renew the covenant is to develop spiritual practices that relate us to the exercise of faith in the modern world. What the writer to the Hebrews would say, and probably Dr. Leet would also, is that it is all of the above. He would say that we are standing in a covenant relationship with God that can be manifested in many ways, but what is important to understand is that it is this intimate relationship which God initiated through the work of our Lord Jesus Christ. What is so important is to know that what God started in us has been God's doing, and we respond in faith and love.

A New Priest

What adds to the certainty of what God makes readily available to us is that the Lord Jesus Christ acts and is our great or High Priest over the house of God. The writer indicates that the Lord Jesus Christ performs the same functions for us the priest was called to perform on behalf of the Hebrew people. The priest was the one who made the sacrifice for the people. That sacrificial system was in no way intended to be the sacrifice which people would make to pay for their sins, ameliorate God toward them, or appease God in some form or fashion. The sacrifice was acted out in front of the people by the priest so they could see that God provided the sacrifice for them to atone for their sins.

75

Jesus performed the sacrifice for us by offering himself upon a cross. This was God's furnished sacrifice for us to give final, conclusive, lasting, and eternal evidence that God has forgiven the sins of the world. So likewise, the Priest Jesus was called to enter the sanctuary of God, as only the priest could do for the people, to intercede for us. The priest made the prayers for the people. The priest was the assurance that God was ready to hear of the needs of the people. Now all of that is incorporated in what the Lord Jesus has accomplished for us as the Priest over the whole house of God, which means the extent of God's rule. We have more than a foot in the door of God. We have more than just a friend who can put in a good word for us. We have a whole new approach to God, because God made the approach to us through God's Son, our Lord. That is what it means to say that we can approach "God because we have a great priest over the house of God." On this day we remember that our priest made the once-for-all sacrifice on our behalf that we might always have free access to God. None of this makes sense unless one realizes how desperately important this was for us to have Jesus do this for us.

Let Us Approach With A True Heart

Because we have Christ as our High Priest working for us and we have access to God, the writer goes on, "Let us approach with a true heart in assurance of faith, with our hearts sprinkled clean from an evil conscience and our bodies washed with pure water." The atoning work of our Lord through the cross makes it possible for us to approach God in the worst of circumstances. A good case in point of the free access to the throne of God is Frank McCourt's account of his youth in *Angela's Ashes*. Growing up in dire poverty in an Irish home, Frank also grew up with poor notions of what God is like. Named after St. Francis of Assisi, Frank comes to that moment when he completely disowns any faith in the good St. Francis. On his sixteenth birthday he is brimming with guilt. He got drunk on his first pints of ale furnished by his uncle the night before. He hit his mother in the face and accused her of infidelity to his absent father. He senses guilt for having sent his teenage love, a patient with consumption, to her grave and hell. He curses St. Francis for his failure to help children in poverty as well as victims of the Holocaust.

McCourt visits the church of St. Francis to express his anger and disbelief. Father Gregory, a Franciscan priest, asks if he can help the troubled Frank. Frank is convinced Gregory cannot help, because Frank is too sinful even to make a confession. His sins are gross and he has no faith. Patiently the priest assures Frank that Christ has died for his sins, that God loves him, and before she died God forgave Theresa with whom Frank had shared his sexual trysts. After absolution, prayers, and blessings, Frank is able to return to the rainy streets of Limerick in freedom and peace. He had approached God and was washed clean from an evil conscience. Even so, we can approach God with full assurance of faith, knowing that we have been cleansed with the blood of the Lamb.

Holding To The Faith

As God is able to relieve us of any fear, sense of guilt or shame, or any other barrier which would keep us from approaching God, the writer stresses the advice that we "hold fast to the confession of our hope without wavering, for he who has promised is faithful." The writer undoubtedly knows how short-lived our trust can be. One can, and we all do on occasion, walk away from holy absolution only to be caught up in our sins of weakness and shame. Unless we are alert and careful we find ourselves burdened with a load of guilt that can make us timid and fearful that we cannot approach God. In fact, the second and third times around, the guilt can be intensified, because we feel all the more that we have failed God and ourselves. The writer, therefore, encourages us to hold fast to our hope without wavering.

The writer does not suggest we will not sin again. However, in spite of our sinful condition, we should hold fast to the constant hope we have in God as our Savior and Redeemer. The writer says we can do that, because "He who has promised is faithful." God does not go back on the promise. We can approach God again and again. God is always ready to hear and to forgive us. All kinds of people challenge the notion God can forgive again and again. People ordinarily do not find it easy to forgive. Society is unable to contend with civil misbehavior that is repetitious. Religious people often give up on sinners who repeat their offenses. Not so with God. God is able to forgive without interruption or cessation, because God is faithful. God never gives up on the creation or the creature whom God has made. The exception is that God cannot remain faithful to the creature who fails to believe in God's faithfulness and refuses to turn back to God. That is the irony of the Creator-creature relationship. The creature fails when the creature fails to believe in the goodness of the forgiving God. The writer would say, "Do not let it happen to you. Hold fast to the confession of our hope without wavering."

Provoke Love And Good Deeds

Fortified with the knowledge that we have access to God under all circumstances, but especially in our sinful state, we should be able to act in freedom toward one another. For one thing, we can be accepting of one another as God is accepting of us. We can act out of love, forgiveness, and grace, the same way God acts towards us. The writer says, we "should consider how to provoke one another to love and good deeds." Apart from one another we are apt to find it difficult to act out our faith in service to others. Joined together in a congregation of believers who experience the same gifts of God's love, it is more likely that we will feel the need to act in concert and encourage ways of paying attention to one another's needs as well as to join in common ministries to people in the community as well as in the congregation.

As a congregation we can set goals together and work our ways and means in which we feel the calling to serve the community in love and acts of kindness. The Christian movement from early on gained in strength because of the obvious manner in which Christians felt the need to be of service to the world. Today one item of our national debates is whether the church should not be doing all the works of charity and welfare. That is an interesting phenomenon, because only about forty percent of the population actually belong to religious communities. Also those who lay the burden on the churches like to fault the churches for not having done enough. Those are glaring admissions that the world does not want to provoke its own love and good deeds. At the same time it is also the observation that the Christians can and do act in love and goodness.

Encouraging One Another

In order for Christians to act out of their Christian freedom and state of forgiveness and love, they have to meet together. The writer says that Christians should not neglect meeting together, but encourage one another. We all know that of a given Sunday morning or at some special worship service it is a great encouragement to see good numbers of people sharing the word and sacraments with one another. Most of us take note if a special friend or family member is missing. That is discouragement. However, when we are together, we give special witness to how important our presence is to one another. The writer adds that is especially true for us as we see the Day of our Lord approaching. We all know the sense of accountability we have as the children of God, and it is good encouragement for us to gear up for that day as we help one another along the way. The passion and death of our Lord Jesus Christ make all of these considerations important for us.

The writer began with a contemplation on the sacrifice of our Lord as a new approach to life for all of us. While we mourn on this day the price our Lord had to pay in order to make a new life possible for us sinners, we also call it Good Friday with its joyful remembrance of the significance of our Lord's death. In the Prado Museum in Madrid, Spain, hangs a painting by El Greco portraying our Lord Jesus Christ embracing his cross. The tour guide with passion and special emphasis makes much of the fact that El Greco's interpretation of our Lord carrying the cross was not as though it was burdensome for Christ. Whatever the pain and the burden our Lord suffered, El Greco has overshadowed it with our Lord's warm embrace of the cross he carries. The Christ also looks heavenward with a beatific expression to assure the viewer that our Lord knew his death would be a victory for us to give us free access to heaven. It is this holy assurance the writer to the Hebrews shares with us this day.

Easter Is About You

Probably the most difficult sermon the Christian preacher is assigned to deliver is the sermon for Easter morning. It is common for our Christian congregations to have an overflowing attendance for the festival services. There is high excitement, because the families of the parish also have other activities planned for the day following worship. Children are all agog with the fun attached to bunnies and baskets. The services are replete with extra special music. The pastor may wonder if he will have enough time to get in the usual time for the sermon. All that is distraction enough. However, the real problem for the pastor is to wonder if one is capable of delivering a message that has the convincing power of what Easter really means for us. That should be perfectly understandable. There is absolutely no evidence in any of the Gospels that the first witnesses to the resurrection understood Easter. The reports are that they "disbelieved for joy."

The disciples counted the witness of the women who had been at the tomb as an "idle tale." It went on that way for days, fifty days to be exact, before the disciples caught on. They had to listen to Jesus expound on the Hebrew Scriptures which anticipated Easter. They had to study the Scriptures themselves to see for themselves. Then came the dawning of understanding with the gift of the Holy Spirit at Pentecost. That was the awakening. However, no one, including the disciples, would be convinced about anything simply by hearing that someone came forth from the grave. Easter is far more than that. Easter offers far more than that. That is what the Apostle Paul was getting at in the Second Reading for today. Easter is about you. Easter is about your resurrection. Paul writes, "You have been raised with Christ."

You Have Died

As Paul says, "You have been raised with Christ," he also says, "You have died." The death he writes about is the death you died with Christ. Paul was not talking about the kind of death people talk about when they exclaim, "I could have died!" Such an expression simply describes a shock someone has experienced. The expression usually is as frivolous as the person who says, "I died a thousand deaths," in order to express how stressed the person may have been. There are many flippant expressions about death that are as numerous as the jokes about death. However, some people are obsessed with the concern of death.

Michael Cunningham takes death seriously in his novel *The Hours*. The novel is about Clarissa Vaughan, who is a re-creation of Mrs. Dalloway, the subject of Virginia Woolf's novel of that same name, *Mrs. Dalloway*. Virginia, Clarrisa, and a third woman, Laura Brown, expose the desperation of their lives for love and the unfulfilled desires that make them fit subjects of death. Clarissa meditates on those lives as hours that have passed. They are hours that have been filled with parties, abandoned families, failed loves, and unrealized hopes. Life is so pressured that jumping out of windows, excess of pills, and death by any means is as quiet, easy, and attractive as registering in a hotel. If they do not end their own lives, people die by accident or are slowly devoured by diseases. The best one can make of it is that there is an hour or two, here or there, that offer some ray of hope. Yet everyone knows that the best hours are followed by hours far darker and much more difficult. Clarissa's daughter, Sally, thinks that death and resurrection are intriguing subjects, and it does not seem to matter whether the central character is a hero, a villain, or a clown. Such meditation on death, morbid as it is, touches only the surface and does not match the depths of what the Apostle Paul was thinking when he says that you have died with Christ. For Paul, dying with Christ is not simply recognizing how much death denies life.

You Have Been Raised

What Paul means by our dying with Christ is that we have died to sin. The death to sin is that death which ends the claim sin has on us before God. As sinners we are guilty before God and would be condemned to life without God. Life without God would be eternal death. That death is totally devastating. The women who could think of life only as hours that pass unfulfilled and unrewarding found life so painful that physical death would be a relief from it. Paul would say the opposite. He would say that the life which is so painful because it is unrewarding is only a symptom that those people are dead already. Their physical death would be the complete separation from God. Their death now is their inability to know God as life.

We die in Christ when we acknowledge that we are sinners and that our Lord Jesus Christ died so that in our stead and for our sake he atoned for our sin. Christ's death on the cross was God's statement to the world that God is willing to be reconciled to us if we acknowledge our need for forgiveness by God's grace. At the same time we die with Christ in baptism and by faith we are also raised with him. We are raised to life that is made new in Christ. The life we have in him is life that knows no end. It is the life which is filled with the Spirit of God. It is life that relieves us of the need to justify ourselves or our behavior before God. We know that this life has been made totally acceptable to him. We are regarded as righteous before God. We do not have to prove ourselves. That means we are totally free to do what has to be done.

Think Heavenly

Our death and resurrection in our Lord Jesus Christ have definite implications for us. Because we do not have to be so self-concerned, so worried about our status before God, we can think heavenly. Paul says, "Set your minds on things that are above." Jewel Hilburn, a character in Bret Lott's novel *Jewel,* gives us an illustration of such heavenly thinking. Jewel lives happily in the backwoods of Mississippi with her husband Leston and five children. At age forty Jewel gives birth with great difficulty to a daughter, Brenda Kay. Jewel's life changes radically when she is advised that Brenda Kay is Mongoloid with little hope of living beyond the age of two. Jewel is advised to place the child in institutional care and get on with life with the rest of her family. As she struggles with that possibility and twirls it around in her heart and mind she holds Brenda Kay tightly in her arms. She whispers to herself over and over again portions of Psalm 139, "Whither shall I go from Thy Spirit? Or whither shall I flee from your presence? If I ascend into heaven, Thou art there; if I make my bed in hell, behold Thou art there." Jewel knows there is more to the psalm but she concentrates on the phrase, "Thou art there." She is not sure how God is dealing with her, but she concentrates on the presence of God, regardless of how she chooses. God is present, and she knows she can make her decision in the light of that Presence. She is thinking heavenly.

No doubt many of us here have reflected on that psalm under the same kind of pressures as Jewel experienced. We may also have thought of the line from the hymn "Abide With Me:" "I need your presence every passing hour." To set our "minds on things that are above" is not to think about harps, angels, and comfortable clouds. Rather it is to think things through as the people of God who are blessed with the presence of God in all our doings. We know God's presence not only in the troubled times, but as we go about our daily business and routines. One translation of Paul has it, "Be heavenly minded." That is a memorable way of thinking about it. As we roll up our sleeves and get to work in the grubby everyday stuff we are called to do, we can be "heavenly minded."

Don't Be Grounded

As Paul encourages us to be heavenly minded, he also adds, "Set your minds on things that are above, not on things that are on the earth." That is hard to do. How in all the world are we going to get along on this earth if we do not think about the things of the earth? What Paul would answer is that he was not encouraging us to ignore everything that is around us, particularly those things for which we are responsible. What he is suggesting is that we not permit the things in this world to control our lives. We are not to become slaves to the creation nor the things within the creation.

In E. L. Doctorow's novel *The City Of God,* there are incidents and persons that seem unrelated. However, the intention of the novel is to show how they are related. The situations portrayed appear to be related by the absence of God or the unwillingness of God to reveal God's presence in life.

One meditation in Doctorow's book contemplates how vast the universe has become for us. The more that we learn about the creation, the more advanced we are in the management of the universe, the more remote God appears to be. That seems to be the case in theology itself. Father Tom Pemberton, an Episcopal priest, gives up on trying to make sense out of his theological study and resigns from the priesthood. He marries Sarah Blumenthal, a Hebrew rabbi with whom he uncovers names of persons responsible for the Holocaust in Poland. At his wedding, the former priest, known as Pem, speaks a prayer in which he challenges God to make up for the lapses in God's attention to all the catastrophes taking place in the world. He suggests that God remake us and that we remake God. The novel closes with a meditation on the future of the city of God. In reality it is a meditation on the city of Man, which will undergo utter physical, emotional, economic, and political confusions that can only create more military totalitarian abuse. That is a good description of how things are when people set their minds on the things on the earth. The human situation without the presence of God creates chaos.

Your Life Is Hidden

The irony is that God has done what Tom Pemberton prays for in his wedding prayer. God has reinvented himself in the Person of Jesus of Nazareth, who became one of us to die and rise again for us, so that we can understand God's love for a fallen world. In Christ, God also reinvents us, as we die and rise again in Christ. The fact that we have died and risen with the Lord Jesus Christ by faith in holy baptism means that our lives are "hidden with Christ in God." That may sound like strange language to us. However, when you meditate on that powerful notion you realize how meaningful this is in our lives. Paul is impressing upon us the fact that God is present in the world in and through us. It is in us that the power of God moves. Paul says that is a "hidden" life in Christ, because that is not how the world sees it. For the world the power is concentrated in city hall, the governor's office, and the White House. Power is located on Wall Street and in our giant corporations which effect bigger and larger mergers to concentrate the power even more. For all of that, what has all this great power achieved in ridding the world of violence, hatred, prejudice, racism, anti-Semitism, and war? What has all the power in the world done to feed the hungry, clothe the naked, and give shelter to the homeless?

Yet the powers for reconciliation, forgiveness, grace, mercy, and genuine charity are concentrated in the people of God, the faithful of our Lord Jesus Christ. They go about their work quietly, faithfully, and effectively in their own homes, in their vocations, and in the society. They are the real glue in the society. They give of themselves and of their possessions to relieve pain, hurt, and want in the world. The world does not recognize and salute these followers of Christ as the great heroes in the society. They appear to be powerless, meek, and mild in the face of *Fortune* magazine's picks for the most powerful among the wealthy influential people of the world. The people whose lives are hidden in Christ, however, move in and among the world as the people who guarantee the presence of God within the creation and the society.

When Christ Is Revealed

The reason the Apostle Paul wrote this letter to the congregation at Colossae was because there was evidence that some teachings alien to the gospel of our Lord Jesus Christ had been circulating in the congregation. Paul sensed that these teachings were an attempt to make some kind of hybrid of the Christian faith and the Greek philosophy about the universe. People had been attracted to the teachings about a hierarchy of "elemental spirits of the universe," angelic beings who were to be worshiped. These beings were ranked in authority and were to offer some form of reconciliation between humanity and the gods. These teachings represented a blending of astrology and philosophy emerging in ethical regulations of the people's behavior. Paul labeled these teachings simply as human commands offered in the "appearance of wisdom promoting self-imposed piety" (2:23). Paul urged his people to ignore the efforts to make them captive to this "empty deceit" and "human tradition" (2:8). Paul recognized that these instructions were ineffective in dealing with the core problem of self-indulgence. Worse than that, they were antithetical to the work of our Lord Jesus Christ.

Paul did not need to waste time arguing about the existence or non-existence of forces in the universe. What Paul did know was that the fullness of the universe is revealed in the Person of our Lord Jesus Christ who is Lord of all and in whom we have died to whatever forces are out there that try to control us. What was obvious in the popular notions of the relationship of the human to the cosmos, or the universe, was that somehow the gods had to be favorable to the creatures. Paul discards the human efforts to suggest how this could happen. What Paul proclaims is that it has already happened in the manner in which our Lord died and rose again to be revealed in us. Now, our lives are already hidden in Christ, there will come that day when Christ will be fully revealed.

It Will Be In Glory

To be sure at the present it is not obvious to the world that our lives are hidden in Christ, but we know it is so, because Paul says, "Christ ... is your life." We know that Christ is present because we understand ourselves, the creation, history, and the daily news in the light of what Christ is to us. We know that our lives are God's gift to us, and the new life God has given us in Christ Jesus is all of life redeemed. That is basic stuff. For us it is a tragedy that the world cannot understand itself this way. This is why we read history with all of its great tales of human knowledge, ingenuity, creativity, technology, and artistry as failure in its inability to solve the great problems of human relations. However, in faith we live in high hope of that day when the Lord of the Creation will be revealed in glory. It is then that we, too, will be revealed in glory with him.

Glory in Christ is what we celebrate anew this Eastertide. It is a fortunate innovation in the liturgical calendar that we no longer

87

refer to the Sundays which follow Easter as the "Sundays after Easter," as though Easter is over. We now call them the "Sundays of Easter." This innovation encourages us to allow the insights of the Sundays of Easter to wash over us until we understand the full implications of what Christ has done and is still doing for us. There was no celebration of glory that first Easter. The disciples fell all over themselves trying to get the import of the day. For us, too, we need much time to contemplate the power and effect of the fact that the Christ, who Paul says is "seated at the right hand of God," lives also within us to serve with us until that day he is revealed in glory and we along with him. Until that day, we can take seriously the advice of the Apostle to "seek the things that are above" serving in humility and being "heavenly minded."

The Outcome Of Faith

The United States of America has earned the reputation of being the most violent culture in the world. That really is an oxymoron. How can one speak of culture as being violent? Yet the problem of violence is so widespread in our nation that Gavin De Becker, an authority on violence, notes that we are a nation with more firearms than adults, and twenty thousand guns enter our commerce every day. His book, *The Gift of Fear,* is about our fear which furnishes us survival signals to protect us from violence. We should not be shocked that anyone is capable of violence. The psychiatrist Karl Menniger said he did not believe in the criminal mind, because everyone's mind can produce criminal thoughts. Freud and Einstein once exchanged notes on violence. Einstein wrote that man has in himself the need to destroy.

De Becker's book is to help people develop an awareness of how their own intuitions can make them alert to how they can protect themselves when the threat of violence in any form is present. This is a very important book for our day. If we are to be equipped to handle this major problem, we must be grateful for a knowledge of the human situation and the gift of fear. At the same time we also get help from another direction. In the Second Reading appointed for today we hear the Apostle Peter explain what resources we have in the gift of our faith in dealing with the problems we must face in the world. The Apostle gives a good description of how we can rely upon the protection God affords us through the faith God furnished us in Christ our Lord.

A Living Hope

The word which we have in the Second Reading is an excerpt from the First Epistle of Peter. What is significant about the letters from Peter is that he writes with great confidence about the faith. Remember this is the same Peter who started to sink when our Lord permitted him to walk on the water. This is the same Peter who had been so brash as to boast that he would die with our Lord rather than to deny him. Yet he was the one who cowardly caved in and denied any relationship with Jesus when a maid suggested that he had been a disciple of our Lord. Peter had been thoroughly chastened by that experience. He had been forgiven and reinstated by the Risen Christ. Out of the experience of God's grace Peter could write firsthand about the hope that is ours in Christ. By the initiation into the power of forgiveness and grace Peter became known as the Apostle of Hope. He could write, "Blessed be the God and Father of our Lord Jesus Christ! By his great mercy he has given us a new birth into a living hope through the resurrection of Jesus Christ from the dead." Note again: we experience "a new birth into a living hope."

The hope we have is not something belonging only to the future. Now we have a hope that is alive and is working for us. We have hope like Peter, who was the shaken, frightened, tearful spectacle running from the palace of the high priest, who woke to the news on Easter day that his Lord was alive. The Lord at the seashore publicly forgave Peter and made a new man of him. So it was Peter who also rose from sin and shame to live life anew. We share that experience with Peter each day as we confess our sins and pray that God forgive us. Each day we are born anew as we know we are forgiven. That is a living, lively hope we have. We can have life restored and renewed each day by the God against whom we have sinned. God gives us the hope and the courage to live and manage our lives in spite of the fact that we know all too well how our weaknesses and our frailty can be a drag on our daily lives. Good intentions are not enough. We need to know God can and still does use us.

An Imperishable Inheritance

Not only has God given us a living hope as daily assurance for us of God's grace, but our future is also assured. Peter can say the resurrection of Jesus Christ confers on us "an inheritance that is imperishable, undefiled, and unfading." It is significant how the Apostle felt compelled to describe the inheritance we receive through Christ is "imperishable, undefiled, and unfading." In our language today, we might say, "uncontested." One might feel uncomfortable about the business of having to write a will to designate the distribution of one's estate. However, every lawyer could tell you that the best of families have been torn apart by squabbles over contested inheritances. Then, too, the performance of heirs who inherit great fortunes generally is not exemplary. Many inheritances have been squandered like the fortunes which slip so often from the hands of those who win the lotteries. Or lives may have been ruined by the inheritances some heirs have received.

Doris Duke, the world famous heir of the Duke tobacco empire fortunes, led a lonely, miserable, and psychotic life, because her father had warned her that people would always be after her money. She was super sensitive to the fact that people did not like her for her own person, but only because of her wealth. The Apostle Peter wants us to be sure that the inheritance we receive has none of the flaws, temptations, weaknesses, or bad effects that worldly inheritances have. This inheritance is made sure and effective for us by the source from whom it comes. Our Lord Jesus, the Risen Christ, is the One who is the guarantor of our inheritance. The inheritance is imperishable, because Jesus made good on the last will and testament he wrote with his own blood and verified by his resurrection to establish its distribution.

Reserved In Heaven

As certainly as the Apostle Peter wanted us to be assured that we are the heirs of an imperishable inheritance, he also added that this inheritance is "kept in heaven" for us. Of course, the heavens in Peter's day were known as the realm of the gods. This is meant to say to us that we shall dwell in the presence of God. In our day it is more difficult to point to the sky and speak of the heavens.

Our young people know all about space and the infinity it suggests. There is no way we can become literalistic in describing the heaven or the space in heaven which is being kept for us. What we can say is that we know that we shall be in the presence of our Risen Lord Jesus Christ. Peter's purpose in sharing this good news with us was not to offer a bromide to hold us over until we get to heaven. He was being far more practical than that.

Because our inheritance has been guaranteed and we have a place with God, this enables us to act freely. We should not have to be concerned or worried about those matters. They have been settled. We know we now are a part of the company of heaven. We are free to serve and wait on others rather than to try to win heaven by giving our undivided attention to ourselves. It is like a young person who has the freedom of knowing that the inheritance awaits. That person has the freedom of choosing to serve in life without the burden of worrying about how the future is going to work out. To be sure, the young heir who does see the advantage of that good fortune could be a wastrel and make nothing of life. The one who understands the benefits is free to explore life, to make it interesting, to give of oneself completely for the sake of others or for a meaningful cause. Peter would certainly want us to understand that. However, Peter perceived the blessing of our inheritance in Christ as a deeper and more profound way of understanding life. Being realistic about life, Peter saw the advantages of our relationship with God as being very special.

Protected By God's Power

Peter did not confine the advantages of being heirs to the inheritance in heaven as only being inspired to serve under the conviction that our future is secure. He adds that we are "being protected by the power of God through faith for a salvation ready to be revealed in the last time." Peter is saying God is actively working in our lives to keep us in the true faith. Luther would say the same. In an explanation of the Third Article of the Creed concerning the Holy Spirit, Luther says that God not only calls us and enlightens us in the faith, but then God keeps us in the faith. That takes a lot of doing. There are all kinds of forces out in the world that work against the faith. Those who have grown up in the faith can recall how simply and quietly one could learn about the faith and accept the profound truths about God's grace and love in the most trusting manner. However, as we grow older each phase of our lives brings new disturbances, new ideas, new doubts, and new fears that are hindrances and threats to the faith.

As certainly as those challenges to the faith come, God is present to strengthen, guard, and protect us against those enemies of the faith. In word and sacraments God is willing to strengthen us through faith. God is ready and willing to go all the way with us. God is willing to guard and protect us with divine power to see us through to the end in the same way God guarded and protected our Lord Jesus Christ. Peter puts it this way. God is willing to protect us by power "through faith for a salvation ready to be revealed in the last time." We will get to see the results of our faith in the same way our Lord Jesus was revealed as victor over sin and death. Peter, who was one of the Twelve, describes the experiences of faith in the same way faith had to work in the life of Jesus. We are always exposed to a tried and true method in the life of our Lord. Faith is the proof positive that God is working for us.

Joy For Tough Times
Peter says that ought to be enough to rejoice about. Yet Peter adds more. We can rejoice in the fact that God is present to guard and protect us in the faith. That is true even in the worst circumstance. Peter writes, "In this you rejoice, even if now for a little while you have had to suffer various trials." That is the way it is. Life is filled with all kinds of bumps and bruises, hardships and trials. There is no escaping that. Peter knew that well. Peter did not have to invent or add troubles in order to try to make a point. The fact of the matter is that there are troubles in the lives of every one of us. Just like the demonic forces that attack, belittle, and threaten us, various other trials come along to test the faith. Peter says, "The genuineness of your faith — being more precious than gold that, though perishable, is tested by fire."

Trials and troubles, whether they are health, economic, or emotional traumas, can wear on the faith like the worst kind of demonic enemy. We certainly can realize there are tests for the most precious gift we have, our faith. We can get it straight. We can employ our faith to deal with these various trials and treat them as being only temporary, no matter how long they last. Or we can give up on the faith and let the troubles and hardships take over and destroy the faith. When we let faith be the means by which we deal with and handle the troubles and the trials, then, Peter says, our faith "may be found to result in praise and glory and honor when Jesus Christ is revealed." Once again our faith is identified with our Lord Jesus Christ. Edward Schillebeeckx, a Roman Catholic theologian, wrote an excellent text on the nature of Jesus. The book is called *Jesus*. In it he explains that it is a mistake to think formulas about Jesus are the faith. We must understand that Jesus, the Son of God, identified himself as One who could call God "Abba," so that we, too, can call God "Abba" by faith under the worst trials.

Love Positive

Schillebeeckx implies it is important for us to understand how Jesus made his real identity known by being able to call God "Abba." As the Son of God, Jesus could call on God as Father. As a true human being, in prayer or distress, Jesus called on God as Abba, that is, Father. God would deliver him. Peter would want us to appreciate that the love between the Father and the Son revealed as God's love for the world is the hope which Peter describes for us. Peter maintains that the same relationship which exists between the Father and the Son is what we experience in Christ. Peter writes, "Although you have not seen him, you love him; and even though you do not see him now, you believe in him and rejoice with an indescribable and glorious joy."

Most of us find Peter's language familiar. We may talk the same way about cherished deceased parents who continue to have a powerful influence in our lives. As we reflect on what they have contributed to us, we love them all the more, even though they may have been gone from us for many years. We may feel the same way about dear teachers or professors who have left indelible imprints upon our lives. We may have been removed from them for many years, yet we love them as though they were ever present. Or there could be people in a variety of professions who may be models for us. We may never have met them, nor ever have seen them, but we are grateful for their contributions to our lives. Peter recognizes our Lord Jesus Christ as the one who has done the most for us. We know our Lord as our Shepherd, Redeemer, Savior, Teacher, Friend, and our God. Though we have not seen him, we live on intimate terms with him through the word and sacraments and prayer. This intimacy is nourished through the sacrament in which we know his presence in a unique fashion. We receive him by faith and know his presence for us. He becomes a part of our very being. Like Peter we can say we "believe in him and rejoice with an indescribable and glorious joy."

The Outcome

We began this discourse with an appreciation for the thesis of Gavin De Becker, who says we should take advantage of "the gift of fear" for living in a violent culture. One can certainly agree that our fear can produce "survival signals which protect us from violence." Riding home in the evening one regularly hears the screech of sirens that move on to tragedy wrought by violent people. The recital of abusive treatment of men as well as women and children is monotonous. One wonders how tired God must be of looking in on the human situation. Our own intuition should warn us how fallen the world is and that we must be alert to defend ourselves against these threats of explosive people.

At the same time, we have the good word from the Apostle Peter that in this messed up creation we have divine protection of another sort. As we face various trials we must endure with suffering, we are guarded by the power of God through faith. As we heard the Apostle explain the advantages faith in our Lord Jesus Christ work for us, he assures us that we can live with confidence and joy. Peter concludes you can have this joy, "for you are receiving the outcome of your faith, the salvation of your souls." Our salvation is not only that we have the inheritance reserved for us in heaven. Right now we enjoy the blessing of knowing our salvation is working for us as the means of coping with, defending against, and overcoming whatever suffering and trials we have coming our way. Viewed that way, we can understand why Peter says it'll be only "for a little while."

Genuine Mutual Love

A rather insightful novel about the problem of Christian missions to Africa is Barbara Kingsolver's story *The Poisonwood Bible*. Kingsolver weaves her story around Nathan Price, a fundamentalist, legalistic preacher who takes his wife and four daughters to serve in the heart of the Belgian Congo. While they are there, in 1960 Patrice Lumumba emerges as the leader of his people when Belgium grants the Congolese their independence. Soon after, Mobuto comes to power. Nathan Price decides to remain and serve with his family even when the resources of his sponsors are cut off. As one missionary stated, people fled the Congo for many reasons. They left for common sense, lunacy, or faintness of heart. However, he also added that some remained for the same reasons. Nathan's wife and daughters relate their observations of how things happened in this troublesome transition time in the Congo. What they watched and experienced struck them all differently and evoked different reactions to the Congolese scene as well as to the die-hard approach to missions by their father.

In reading this fascinating story one has to raise the inevitable question of the wisdom of the rule of foreign powers who abused their practice of colonialism in Africa. At the same time we have trouble accepting the rise of native factions who are not trained or schooled in democratic rule. More important for us, as Christians we have to be concerned about the identity of so much mission work with the abuses of colonialism. Even more crucial is the fact that so much evangelization in the name of Christ, overseas or at home, is not based on the gospel of grace but on legal approaches to culture. In contrast to that, we have in the Second Reading for this day a carefully crafted Christian approach to change.

The Context

The context for the Second Reading is the approach of persecution of the Christian communities under Nero. It is the Apostle Peter who writes this exhortation to the Christians to be prepared for the worst, but at the same time, to be confident in the face of trial. Some scholars do not believe Peter wrote the letter, because of its highly sophisticated Greek. The average pastor who reads the Greek New Testament with some ease will have trouble with the Petrine epistles. However, it could well be that Sylvanus, who is mentioned in the last chapter, could have written the letter at Peter's behest as Peter surmises that his own martyrdom might be imminent. Just how it happened, we cannot be sure.

What is impressive is the fact that Peter's letter was addressed to Gentile Christians, who did not have a long tradition in Christianity to fall back on. As members of young congregations they had to rely upon the faith, as they had come to know it, to muster the strength to face trial and persecution. The letter reflects that kind of insight. The author assures the readers they will be able to face what they must. They are not to feel abandoned or doomed. This studied approach stands in rich contrast to what Kingsolver portrays as the shabby and unsubstantial methods often applied in areas like the Congo. What is important for us is that what Peter applies in a time of uncertainty for the early Christians is important for us. Fortunately, for us, we are not threatened with persecution of the faith by our government. Yet Christians in some parts of the world are threatened by persecution. At the same time, our faith may be intimidated and threatened by other forces within the world. In the face of that fact, all of us can use the kind of encouragement for our faith offered by the Apostle Peter in such a thoughtful way. Peter makes the best use of the resources of the faith to build a good case for us.

Your Accountability

The section of Peter's letter assigned for this day begins with an exhortation for us to be accountable to God for our actions. This follows upon a longer statement which reminds us we have the same obligations incumbent upon the people of God in the days of the prophets. The warning is that people who know the revelation of God in Christ Jesus should not be conformed to the desires of this world. Rather we should remember that the word holds true for us as it did for people from the beginning. God says, "You should be holy, even as I am holy." Because our Creator has the authority to make this demand of us, Peter urges us to recognize when we call upon God for anything, we have no legs to stand on. God is our Judge, and God judges "all people impartially according to their deeds." Putting it frankly, Peter writes, "Live in reverent fear during the time of your exile."

When Peter uses the term "exile," he means the time we have in this world. Peter uses this term because he uses illustrations from the life of the children of Israel who lived in the exiles of Egypt and Babylon. Peter wants us to know we live in the freedom of the gospel of God's grace. However, at the same time, so long as we are in this world, we must think of our time here as something of an exile from the home and life we know will be in heaven with God. Also while we are in this world, we should know the temptations of unbelief and rebellion are always there. We can never become flip about our relationship with God. We must know that whenever we think we have it made with God on our own, God can come down on us as an angry Judge.

The Example In Israel

It is not Peter's intention, however, to dwell on the possibility of our loss of status with God. He reminds us the possibility of our fall from grace is always there. However, what he emphasizes is that God does everything to assure us such a possibility does not have to occur. In the face of the worst chaos and turmoil, we know we can be secure with God. He recalls the manner in which God did deal with the ancient people Israel. From the manner in which Peter writes, we can assume that the Gentile Christians may have known about the history of the children of Israel from their dealings with the Jewish people. Or they may have been instructed by Christian teachers in the Hebrew history. Either way, Peter assumes they know as we also should know.

Peter writes, "You know that you were ransomed from the futile ways inherited from your ancestors." The futile ways were the sacrifices of animals. Those sacrifices did not do anything to win God's favor. What the sacrifices did was to assure the people they did not have to be sacrificed themselves or sacrifice others. God loved the people, and the sacrificial system of the Hebrews was the sign that God loved them in a way that no other god could love. Christ came to replace the sacrificial system. Jesus offered himself to take the place of the sacrificial system, so that we also can be sure there is no need for sacrifice. Jesus shed his blood as the Lamb without defect or blemish not to appease God but to demonstrate God's love for us. To make the case even more sure, Peter writes that Jesus was destined for this role before the foundation of the earth. And now God raised Jesus from the dead to prove the point. Because of that, Peter says you now "trust in God, who raised him from the dead and gave him glory, so that your faith and hope are set on God." What God did in both the sacrificial system of the Hebrew era and in the death of our Lord Jesus Christ was to make it possible for people to believe and trust in God. That is what had been lost by the creature within the creation. This was God's great recovery act. God gave the evidence of divine and eternal love for us.

The Example Of Slave Masters

While Peter used the example of the replacement of the Hebrew sacrificial system, he expanded on the freedom our Lord Jesus Christ has won for us by using the language from the slave market. Peter's Christian audience included many people who were either slaves or had been slaves. What they could understand, whether they were free or slave, was the language that described manumission, the freeing of slaves from the legal bonds of slavery. Masters could buy or sell slaves. Someone could buy from a master the freedom for a slave by paying a price. Peter mixes the metaphor. Peter talks about being ransomed from the sacrificial system with the blood of Christ. Not only is the metaphor mixed, but we do not get to know to whom the price or ransom is paid. Certainly, Jesus does not pay a ransom to God for us. God is the one who sent Jesus to set us free. Nor did Jesus pay ransom to sin, the devil, our flesh, death, or hell. It is not important that the analogy is not completed. We all mix our metaphors, and sometimes we cannot take them to their logical conclusions.

What is clear about the illustrations Peter uses is that we are set free. We are no longer slaves to sin, the devil, our flesh, death, or hell itself. Peter does not mention those forces which seek to hold us in their grips. He stresses our freedom from any slavery to which we have been bound. Christ is the one who set us free. Jesus paid the price or the ransom to make that possible. The price our Lord paid was not with "perishable things like silver and gold." Our Lord paid a much higher price. Our Lord paid with his life. He paid with his precious blood. Even though Peter mixes the metaphor and leaves it incomplete, it is music to our ears. It is a declaration of freedom and liberty for us.

A Superior Condition

Peter does not quit with the good word about our freedom and the ability now to trust God. He goes on, "Now ... you have purified your souls by your obedience to the truth." We should recognize this is, indeed, a condition much superior to the way we would live without the freedom God has won for us in Jesus Christ. Our lives have been purified or cleansed by the word of truth. That word of truth is the honesty about ourselves. Without Christ we are condemned sinners who have no way of rescuing ourselves. The word of truth is also that our Lord Jesus Christ has died and risen again for us. The word of truth asserts that in the crucified and risen Christ we become the children of God. We are able to live as free. Peter calls it being "born anew." In Christ our future is secure.

Futurists like James Canton talk about the unlimited potential of the future. There is so much that has been advanced by our technology and the explosion of research and learning that we have to ask if we are prepared for the future. The advances that are now possible in technology, in medicine, in the computerized world, and in space exploration raise questions as to how much we can handle. We also have to ask how we will deal ethically and morally with the problems the world of tomorrow brings. The futurists paint a scenario for us that is purified by the desires for achievement and perfection. However, we know that much of what the futurists predict may not come into being because of the human propensity to abuse, to ruin, to mar, and to destroy much of what should serve our interest and welfare. Tragically it is the human touch that spoils. There once was a cigarette called Old Gold which advertised that its manufacture was "untouched by human hands." That is a dreadful commentary on the human situation. The human touch can be perverse. However, Peter says our future is secure because we "purified our souls by obedience to the truth." We face the future with that confidence. Whether the future would involve the kind of chaos Peter knew persecution would bring, or whether it is personal illness, or the uncertainties of old age, or modern invention and innovation, we are certain of God's presence, grace, and love in whatever circumstances we face.

Freedom To Love

The certainty we know through obedience to the word of truth produces some results besides just feeling good about the future. Peter writes that because our hearts are purified through obedience to the truth, we experience "genuine mutual love," and we can love one another deeply from the heart." The mutual love which we experience is the love of God in Christ Jesus our Lord. It is the Johannine word that emphasizes repeatedly that we love God, because God first loved us (John 15). God's love produces love in our hearts as we respond to the goodness of God's mercy, grace, and forgiveness. We are never bankrupt for the love of God. Our love for God is accepting God's love. The mutuality of our love is triggered by what God initiated in saving and redeeming us. Without God's love we might find it impossible to love.

In the book mentioned in the introduction, *The Poisonwood Bible,* Leah, one of the twin daughters of the fundamentalist missionary in the Congo, is a delightful child in her early teens when they arrive in the Congo. She is the one out of the five females in the family who does the most to please her father. She confesses that she truly tried to set her feet into his footprints. She had faith in her father and love for the Lord. However, her father's insensitivity to the needs of his wife and daughters created doubts and created a void which filled her life with fear. The ability to love is always threatened when there is no mutuality. By contrast, Peter recognized that because of the mutual love we have with God, we are now capable also of "loving one another deeply from the heart." As the people of God we should thrive on the love of God to the point of reflecting this love in the manner in which we love one another.

Guaranteed Product

Peter asserts that we are not only made capable of loving because of our mutual love affair with God, but also what God accomplishes in us with the gift of love has permanent value to it. Peter writes, "You have been born anew, not of perishable but of imperishable seed, through the living and enduring word of God." Peter means what God does for us is not a fly-by-night operation. God does not intend to help us out just for the moment or because God just wants us to feel good. What God starts in us with the gift of faith, whether it was in baptism in infancy, or if we came to the faith in the middle of life or late in life, God wants to take root and hold forever. From God's side of things, God intends that our faith should be indestructible. The word and promise God gives us is imperishable stuff and comes to us through the "living and enduring word." If it does not last, it is not God's fault.

God would keep us strong to all eternity. That is the message which Peter the apostle wanted to get to the people of God whom he knew would soon be suffering persecution under Nero. In the end, tradition has it, Peter himself suffered a martyr's death on the cross in the city of Rome where he labored and the city from which he sent this letter. Tradition also has it that he asked that he be crucified upside down, because he was not worthy to be crucified as our Lord was crucified. A century later the aged Polycarp, Bishop of Smyrna, was arrested and tried. When asked by the proconsul to deny Christ and gain his freedom, he answered "Eighty-six years I have served him, and he never did me wrong; how can I blaspheme my King and Savior?" The tradition yields that he was to be burned at the stake, but when the flames appeared to harm him none, he had to be stabbed to death. Down through the centuries people of God have suffered martyrdom, because they were convinced they were born of imperishable seed. Strengthened by mutual genuine love, they knew they could withstand the trials forced upon them. We can do no less in the face of the trials that may arise out of our serene and prosperous days or in the days of uncetainty and distress. God is feeding us on imperishable stuff of love and grace.

Easter 4
1 Peter 2:19-25

Credit For Suffering

The Second Reading for today is a continuation of readings from the Petrine epistles appointed for the Sundays of Easter. The intention of the first letter of Peter, you recall, is to strengthen the Christians for the persecution coming upon them. In this portion of the letter the subject is undeserved suffering. David Baldacci treats this subject in his novel *The Simple Truth.* This is the story of Rufus Harms, a big black soldier who has served 25 years in a military prison for murder. However, his crime was triggered by experimental drugs the army used on him. He has been notified that he should be free, but he is also aware that those who would be implicated in his unfair treatment would stop at nothing to remove him from the scene. Rufus escapes from a military hospital and is in hiding with his brother Josh. In their idle time in hiding, they talk about their attitudes toward their situation and people.

Josh sizes up all ethnic groups according to their treatment of blacks. He thinks blacks have a gold card privilege from God to hate all whites. Rufus realistically sees all people as God's children and that evil comes in all forms and colors. Rufus refuses to judge people. He knows life is not fair, and as badly as he has been treated, no one is going to take God from him. The official army document which would free him has been sent to the Supreme Court, but it does not appear it has reached the proper people. As dark as his future is, he knows his Savior God is with him. He counts himself a child of God prepared to suffer whatever comes his way. That is what Peter encourages in our reading. However, he also explains why Christians can deal positively with their suffering.

The Context

The chief concern of this apostolic letter is the number of Christians who have to suffer abuse. All Christians must endure suffering of some sort, and the kind word about suffering is applicable to all. However, some were exposed to abuses at the hands of others. To be sure, slaves were the most expendable in that regard. Slaves at this time of writing within the first century were house slaves. Some of them were regarded as part of an extended family. They may have been conquered people who were taken into captivity. If so, they may have been well educated and were bought in order to serve as tutors within the home or as managers of household affairs, or stewards of businesses conducted out of the home. That is why in this letter the Apostle could speak of "kind and gentle masters" who were easier to obey and to accommodate. In that case, the slaves would suffer mostly the lack of freedom to be on their own. There may have also been slaves who sold themselves into slavery for economic reasons. They may have indentured themselves to get a roof over their heads and to have food on the table.

In all cases of slavery, the basic problem was the same. The slaves had no freedom. Yet the Apostle does not play on that theme. The Apostle assumes they understand that they are free before God. Consequently, they had the freedom to act in a way their masters would have no reason to expect. The slaves could act out of a sense of duty not imposed on them by the masters but by the One who had called them to act on God's behalf. Peter suggested the slaves develop a new perspective on work and how to go about their work. The focus was not to be on themselves, but rather on whom they were to serve. To be sure, people do work under different circumstances. Yet Christians can enjoy the fact that they are working with a leg up on most others. From a very human point of view what the Apostle suggests makes good sense.

A Good Example

Peter's suggestion about the behavior of slaves toward their masters, no doubt, did work out well for the slaves. The Apostle Paul offered the same kind of advice. That it did work out well is the case of Philemon and his slave Onesimus. While the apostles did not try to break down the institutions of slavery legally, their Christian advice did eventually work for the welfare and freedom of slaves. That worked also many years later in this country. William Martin writes about it in his historical novel *Citizen Washington*. Jacob, George Washington's slave at Mount Vernon, was married to a slave at another plantation. They had two children, a boy and a girl. One day while Jacob was fishing with his thirteen-year-old son, Jacob encouraged his son to be a good and faithful slave. The son did not accept that well. However, the father suggested he was sure his faithfulness might be rewarded by Mr. Washington, who could purchase Jacob's whole family so that they could all live at Mount Vernon. Match, the son, said that would only keep him enslaved.

Jacob's notion, however, was realized and eventually his family was given manumission. But they elected to work at Mount Vernon, the place they called "home." Jacob's excellent service to his master won him his freedom. The son, however, did run away and did serve with distinction in the Continental Army. His father's advice was not lost on him entirely, though he did always live in fear of being found out. However, it is obvious in the epistle of Peter, that the Apostle wanted to reach beyond what would be good common sense. Peter wants to get beyond the ordinary to highlight how the Christian faith can work even greater wonders. This advice also stretches well beyond the cause of dutiful slaves.

Deserved Suffering

First of all, one has to recognize there is much deserved suffering in the world. Peter writes, "If you endure when you are beaten for doing wrong, what credit is that?" That is easy enough to understand. A child can catch on to that quite early. If one has to go to bed, sit in the corner or whatever for having misbehaved, one cannot brag about taking the punishment. The same is true in school, and later on when one enters into the work force. However, it is also true in many other ways. People may have to suffer because they abuse themselves with poor health habits. We in America are being alerted to that constantly, because we are plagued with self-destructing diet and lifestyles. We think of all the warnings against overeating, workaholism, smoking, alcoholism, and drug abuse, and we just do not see the gains in overcoming these temptations that we would like to see. However, people can also do harm to themselves by not learning to manage their incomes well. Or people can hurt themselves drastically by rude and crude behavior in the work place or at home. These are problems of which all of us can easily be guilty. They are personal pitfalls and dangers into which we can fall easily.

To list the personal problems is not to ignore the larger problems people suffer when they commit the civil crimes, felonies, and social misconduct which bring them civil punishments. Suffice it to say that all of the problems in the world do originate in the minds and hearts of people. Whether they are personal difficulties or sins committed against the society, people are responsible. Peter wants us to acknowledge the kind of judgment that is going on in the world all of the time, and no one can complain about having to suffer or endure it, because it is deserved. That is not easy for us to admit, because much of what we are talking about are difficult to handle ingrained habits. Yet we do well to begin reform at the right places. However, deserved suffering is not what Peter wants to get at. That is almost an aside he mentions in order to get at the subject of undeserved suffering.

Undeserved Suffering

As Peter sweeps aside the topic of deserved suffering or judgment, he moves on to talk about undeserved suffering. He writes, "But if you endure when you do right and suffer for it, you have God's approval. For unto this you have been called." There is a sense in which we all share together in the pain and hardships of the larger society. That is not difficult to understand when we hear of the great catastrophes which can strike at any time in any part of the world. We cringe when we hear about earthquakes taking the property and lives of people wholesale. We suffer when we see families scaling walls and rooftops in order to escape devastating floods. We know how indiscriminate the tornadoes are as they travel paths of wild destruction. Then it is not difficult for us to reach for pen and checkbook, because we know the human suffering involved will reach huge proportions, and though we have been untouched by the misery, in sympathy we suffer with the victims of these dreadful chaotic forces of the creation. The dear people who pay the terrible price have done nothing to whip up these storms of violence. That is undeserved suffering.

However, though Peter would applaud the people who can cope with the travesty nature has loaded on them, he was thinking more about the undeserved suffering that comes to people who are hurt when they do something right. All of us can cite examples of instances when we have helped someone only to have them turn on us. Friends and family members can do that to us. It could also happen when we are trying to serve in church, school, or the community. Before there was a civil rights movement, some people paid dearly when they worked for the acceptance of people of another color in the Christian congregations. The same was true when Christians worked against anti-Semitism. Peter would say we have a calling to endure that kind of suffering for the sake of the good. Well, there are many other forms of wrongful suffering to be endured.

Other Kinds Of Wrongful Suffering

If employee endurance of wrongful suffering is high, the dockets of the small claims courts will offer how much people witness to the fact that they suffer wrongfully at the hands of their neighbors. At one time Geneva, Switzerland, had the reputation among tourists of being a city where the customer was always wrong. Today the customers in America complain more and more about the improper and poor treatment they receive from automatic answering machines of the companies they must deal with. The customers can suffer wrongfully at the hands of the automated clerks and service managers. However, that kind of wrongful suffering is minor compared to what Peter had in mind. Peter was preparing Christians to deal with the wrongful suffering they might have to endure for the sake of the faith they confessed in our Lord Jesus

Christ. The Apostle knew the occasional and intermittent persecution Christians suffered would become more general and more widespread. The growing persecutions would introduce prolonged and fatal suffering. Suffering for the sake of the faith or for the gospel was neither controversial or contestable. It would be just plain wrong and all the more difficult, because the people suffering would be obviously on God's side. One could explain why such suffering takes place because of the nature of the enemies of the gospel who caused it.

Peter does not treat it here, but we could add the inexplicable kind of suffering that occurs with birth or congenital defects, handicaps, rare diseases, plagues, and epidemics. We could add the environmental catastrophes like tornadoes, hurricanes, and earthquakes. We can throw into the hopper of suffering the pain, the hurt, and the cost of accidents that occur from recklessness, violence, neglect, error, and poor judgment at the hands of people. Everyone can probably come up with more examples and instances of pain and suffering caused by the failure of machines, implements, and technocratic instruments. The Apostle would have no objection to our addition of the many forms of undeserved suffering we have noted, because we know his counsel would be the same for all.

The Model For Suffering

What Peter offers as consolation for those who suffer undeservedly is the model of our Lord Jesus Christ. He writes, "If you endure when you do right and suffer for it, you have God's approval. For to this you have been called, because Christ also suffered for you, leaving you an example, so that you should follow in his steps." That sounds strange for an Apostle. That would change Christ into a norm or standard, an ideal hero whom we should follow. Back in the twenties Charles Sheldon wrote a novel called *In His Steps*. The story made the gospel into a law, Jesus being a hero or model for behavior to follow. That has become a trend again with people asking the question, "What would Jesus do?" Peter did not suggest that. If Jesus were only a model of

110

behavior, answers how to behave would still be debatable and controversial.

What Peter suggests is that Jesus was a model of faith. He adds, "You should follow in his steps. 'He committed no sin, and no deceit was found in his mouth.' When he was abused, he did not return abuse; when he suffered, he did not threaten; but he entrusted himself to the one who judges justly. He himself bore our sins in his body on the cross, so that, free from sins, we might live for righteousness; by his wounds you have been healed." Jesus is our model for suffering in the manner in which he believed. Peter indicates he was not vengeful in any way, and he did not have to be. He could trust the Heavenly Father, knowing God had made things right when God raised Jesus from the dead and vindicated him. That is how Jesus is the model. He made it possible for us to trust, believe, and rely upon God in the worst of circumstance, in the face of death itself.

The Presence Of God

The Presence of our healing, redeeming, providential, and eternal God makes it possible for us to receive credit for suffering patiently in faith without a sense of vengeance. A good parable on how faith works in the time of suffering without vengeance is difficult to find. We recognize how common it is for people to expect vengeance or pay back for some abuse they have suffered. People expect justice to be the correction of abuses they may have received verbally, physically, materially, and emotionally. Regularly we read and hear about the cases that involve the trauma of mental cruelty. We can recognize the desirability of jury trials for those bringing suits for vengeance, because they know that juries themselves find some delight in leveling judgment against those who are the abuser. Revenge and vengeance is a built-in goal of the society. Small children begin early with their protestations about "being fair."

It should be obvious to us, however, that the urge for vengeance can be as destructive as whatever urge created the abuse in the first place. People who carry the burden of seeking vengeance have their lives soured by their need to get back at those who have hurt or wounded them. To be freed of that attitude is a great relief indeed. Our Lord did his level best to make that possible for us. By his death and resurrection he made it possible for us to rise to a higher life in him. That is how the Apostle Peter concludes it for us. "For you," he writes, "were going astray like sheep, but now you have returned to the shepherd and guardian of your souls." On our own in our suffering, pain, and panic we are apt like sheep to run in any direction. However, it is our faith in our time of suffering that leads us back to the Shepherd who holds us in his everlasting arms. As Peter said in the beginning of this pericope, "For it is a credit to you, if being aware of God, you endure pain while suffering unjustly." What this all adds up to is Martin Luther's observation that if you want to know where God is, look to the cross, God is always present in the pain and suffering. God knows our desperate need for the divine presence in the best and the very worst of times.

Identity As A People

Fascinating reading is an account of the Lewis and Clark expedition to the Northwest, titled *Undaunted Courage,* by Stephen E. Ambrose. The saga reveals the importance of this expedition to the Jefferson administration. President Thomas Jefferson had conceived the idea of sending a troop of hardy men to explore the vast territory that stretched from the Missouri all the way to the Pacific northwest. However, the men were not only explorers who were to return with scientific data from this vast territory. The band of brave stalwarts were to serve as emissaries of good will to the native populations they would find along the way. President Jefferson sent a message of good will in which he promised that the great white father to the east would incorporate these peoples into an organized manner of living together as one people.

Lewis had a lengthy, prepared speech he tried to share with each new tribe of native Americans he encountered. One can appreciate how tense these meetings could be. Some meetings were more cordial than others. Some were hostile. Obviously, the meetings were not simply get acquainted times. Nor were they merely curiosity hours or show-and-tell sessions. What was deeply involved was an understanding of one another's cultures, and whether they could survive side by side. It was a probing for trust and mutual understanding. If you can appreciate what was involved in those kinds of meeting, then you can be somewhat sensitive to the message of the Second Reading for today, a portion of the First Letter of the Apostle Peter. In this section of the letter,

113

Peter explains the importance of our understanding of ourselves as a special kind of people.

A Problem

Peter's emphasis is very important. We should understand our identity as the people of God in relationship to others. That is what the Jeffersonian speech read by Lewis was supposed to be. The effort was to show how the people of the Eastern states wanted to be hospitable to the native Americans. However, we all know that the subsequent history was more than tensions between people from the east and the native Americans. Wars were fought as a result of unresolved tensions and animosities. History has been revised in order to help us appreciate the feelings of native Americans and much is being done to right some of the wrongs committed against the native Americans. That is not unique in the annals of history.

The unrest in the Balkan communities results from century old tensions between Muslims and Christians. All of Europe has a checkered history of wars between cultures, because people lacked an appreciation for one another's identity within their religious or secular cultures. Separate languages, customs, and coinage were the barriers between people more than were geographical boundaries. The same stories are repeated for the continents of Africa and Asia, where peoples were separated for the same reasons. Within our own nation, the worst war our country waged was civil strife fueled by differences between peoples over regional, economic, and racial differences. The hardened attitudes of people which develop of their self-understanding as a people die hard. People are separated by their preferences for how they understand themselves and other peoples. Peter knew full well how it would be for Christians as they come to understand themselves as the people of God within a culture in which people have different gods. It was important for them to understand who they were. Peter was very careful to outline for the believers how it is that they come to their identity as the people of God. His approach is noteworthy.

What Peter Did Not Say

In order to understand Peter's approach to the people, we should take the time to note what Peter did not say. Peter did not say anything that would give the believers in our Lord Jesus Christ reason to boast in themselves. Peter did not give reason for the people to wave the flags of triumph or nationalism. Peter laid absolutely no groundwork or basis for claiming racial, ethnic, or cultural superiority. Nor did Peter suggest that the people of God could now enjoy the privilege of sitting in judgment upon all others. There was no suggestion of instilling any attitude in God's people that they should be the people who should cause the kinds of divisions, antagonisms, conflicts, and opposition to others that make for the warring attitudes that raise havoc between the peoples of the earth. In contrast to that, what Peter does suggest is that the people of God should develop a stance that should attract the attention of others to themselves.

Mind you, Peter is writing this at a time when he is aware that believers are enduring persecution under the administration of the Roman Empire by Nero. Peter is aware of the negative and aggressive attitude of the enemies of the Christian faith, yet he does not suggest a hostile position in reaction to what is taking place. Given human standards and behavior, we could expect that it would be perfectly logical to suggest some kind of defensive program that would involve suggestions of active behavior to offset open war on the Christian community. However, at the end of this letter the only resistance Peter encourages is the resistance to the devil himself. The devil busies himself with trying to make unbelievers out of the faithful. Just as he did in the earlier part of this letter, Peter builds up the confidence of the believers so that they can withstand the worst judgments against them.

Non-People

Peter makes his points by reminding the believers whatever good he has to say about them, whatever encouragement he can give them, whatever hope he can hold out to them, they had absolutely no reason to believe in themselves to begin with. Peter reaches back to the history of God's people, the Israelites, for what was analogous to their situation. He says, "Once you were not a people, but now you are God's people; once you had not received mercy, but now you have received mercy." In Egypt the Children of Israel were a non-people. As the descendants of Jacob they had become a large number. But they did not have their own land. They had no leader. They could not rule themselves. They had no boundaries they could describe as their territory. Whatever choice land they had received at one time from the Pharaoh had been taken away from them. They had no civil rights. They were enslaved.

Peter indicates how the believers in our Lord Jesus Christ were in the same predicament. They may have been citizens of the Roman Empire, or they may have been slaves with no civil rights. However, spiritually, they all were slaves of this world. If their claim to identity was that they were Roman citizens or slaves in the Roman world, that would count for naught in the face of death. The Roman world could be conquered, as it later was, and the empire would fall, as it did, and then their identity would be gone. If they were freed from slavery, they would have to find their identity from some other fleeting cause. Likewise, as slave or free, they would receive no mercy from the world, the society, or the government in which they lived when they had to face trials, tribulation, and the ultimate judgment of death. That is the final test of who we are and what we can expect. The measure of what our lives have been is how we will be judged in the face of the One who created us. In preparing the believers for the test of persecution, Peter prepared them to meet their God.

Like Babes

Peter is careful to help his audience understand that because they have moved from being no people to become the children of God, they should not think that they are suddenly spiritually so mature that they handle things on their own. Peter thinks just the opposite. He writes, "Like newborn infants, long for the pure, spiritual milk, so that by it you may grow into salvation — if indeed you have tasted that the Lord is good." Christians should know they always have room for growth. They always can learn more. They always can grow in the experience of the goodness of God.

The metaphor that Peter uses is especially apropos. We think of how a newborn infant has come into the world to draw in the first breath on its own, then move into the warmth of the mother's embrace and to take its first taste of food from the mother's breast. Immediately the child senses the dependence upon the goodness of the mother.

Peter says that is our story spiritually. We have come to new life in our Lord Jesus Christ and tasted of the goodness of God. Now we should continue to long for that spiritual food that God gives so freely that we might continue to grow spiritually. We are never fully grown spiritually. We have never reached our potential in experiencing what God is willing to give us. That is why we keep coming back to this altar to taste of God's goodness in the sacrament. We keep coming back to sit and hear the word of God's grace and forgiveness proclaimed week after week. That is why we can never tire of the opportunities to learn more at the feet of teachers who share the word of grace with us.

Like Stones

Peter adds to the comforting picture of us as babes thriving on the milk of God's word to speak of us as stones being built into a spiritual house with the Lord Jesus. "Come to him, a living stone, though rejected by mortals yet chosen and precious in God's sight." Jesus is that living stone whom the builders rejected who has become the chief cornerstone by virtue of his life, death, and resurrection. Now Peter says we are to be the living stones who are built into this spiritual house in which we "offer spiritual sacrifices acceptable to God through Jesus Christ." A good illustration to help us understand Peter's analogy of being chosen as stones for a spiritual building is the Grundtvig National Church in Denmark. The church was started in 1921 and completed in 1941 by seven handpicked masons. The masons, in turn, rejected all bricks that were not perfect. There is an entire community surrounding the church built from the bricks which the masons rejected.

The Apostle Peter would have us understand that though Jesus was rejected to become the chief cornerstone of the spiritual entity we call the church, we have been chosen as living stones, considered now precious in God's sight. We are chosen and precious, because we believe. Peter says that those who believe in our Lord Jesus Christ "will not be put to shame." To us Jesus is the most precious stone. However, Peter adds that those who do not believe continue to find Jesus, our cornerstone, a "stone that makes them stumble and a rock that makes them fall." Peter's comforting illustration of us as living stones is consistent with the manner in which the Apostle Paul uses the same illustration. Paul's emphasis with the illustration is to demonstrate how we fit together to build up this spiritual structure and how dependent upon one another we are in completing the building. Peter uses the metaphor, or analogy, to stress how blessed we are to be chosen to fit into the plan that God has for us. He also makes the contrast with those who fail to make the grade. They are the ones who are discarded and are not employed for the purposes God has in mind for those who love our Lord Jesus Christ

God's Own People

Peter brings his effort at encouragement for his readers to a unique pitch with the words, "But you are a chosen race, a royal priesthood, a holy nation, God's own people." He writes this in contrast to those who stumble over the rock, the cornerstone Jesus. Peter once more calls upon the memories of the special treatment God had for ancient Israel. They were the chosen people whom God had called by the divine intervention in their history. The mystery of their choice could be answered only in the light of God's grace and mercy. Certainly, Israel has no more reason to boast of why God had chosen them any more than we. The question has persisted throughout the history of Israel, "How odd of God to choose the Jews." They were not a world power. Nor could they boast anything wonderful about themselves that God should choose them. Our calling by God is no different. We have nothing to boast of before him.

However, God gave to Israel the priesthood as a means of conveying to them that all they were and had came from the generous and kind hand of God. God approached them through a priesthood so they might approach him through a priestly system. Now our God has approached us through our Great High Priest the Lord Jesus Christ. As a royal, that is, a privileged priesthood, we may go directly to God in prayer and devotion. We may also exercise the right of sharing his word of grace, love, and forgiveness in every way available to us. Peter declares that these privileges qualify us to be a "holy nation." As Israel had been God's special nation through whom God could demonstrate how it is that God is willing to work in history and reveal his hand in the lives of people, God continues God's revelation through us. We are God's people. Our place with God has been made sure through our Lord Jesus Christ.

Proclaimers Of God's Mighty Acts

God chose us as God's people, Peter says, so "we may proclaim the mighty acts of him who called us out of darkness into his marvelous light." There is an old Jewish answer to the question, "Why did God create people?" "Because God loves stories." It is not simply that God needs someone to talk to. It is because God needs someone to recall, relate, and proclaim the wonders of what God has done in the creation and is willing to do in the lives of people. Tragically, there are people who are living in the darkness, that is, people who are blinded to what God has done and is willing to do for people. Peter is convinced that the people of God can show forth the goodness of God under the most trying circumstances.

We have to keep reminding ourselves Peter wrote this remarkable and inspirational letter of hope under the most trying of circumstances. Persecution of the Christians was imminent. Yet Peter knew the power of Rome would ultimately fail. Nations rise and fall. Kingdoms and empires come and go. While history records the greatest and loftiest achievements of people, it discards on the rubbish heap of history peoples, leaders, nations, idols, and conquering heroes who never saw the vision of God's grace and love in Christ Jesus. What Peter could offer to the threatened Christians of his day remains the hope and comfort of all of us who must face the same kind of enemies who intimidate us with different threats. Our enemies may come masked in health, economic, social, temporal, national, or local problems. However intense, subtle, or obvious the enemies are, we know we can face them as the children of God, because we know God is with us to equip us with the resources to deal with whatever we must confront. Peter was right. Nero is now a part of ancient history and crossword puzzles, which identify him simply as the mad fiddler. However, the Church is modern history, very much alive and making new history by proclaiming the mighty acts of God.

The Blessing In Suffering

Toni Morrison wrote the novel *Beloved* to help us appreciate the pain and difficulty blacks had in this country right after the Civil War was ended. One would think freedom would have been especially meaningful for a people who had experienced the burdens of slavery. To be sure, freedom was not only a new but an awesome experience. However, it was also extremely difficult. Imagine having to shape one's career or vocation after having it dictated to you. Imagine trying to adjust to an economy that once treated you as property to be bought and sold. Imagine managing income for the first time in one's life. However, the greatest difficulty of all was to adjust to the society of white people who once owned and abused you. One family discussed the problem seriously. There were those in the family who thought one could relate to the Grangers. They were the people who had owned them. Both Mr. and Mrs. Granger had tried to be nice. However, the objection was that they had been a part of the system. All whites had tolerated the system of slavery. They were all mean and could not be trusted.

The system maintained and used by the whites had been too abusive and too self-serving. If the whites could not see how inhuman the system had been, how could anyone trust them? Our generation is too far removed to be able to appreciate how profoundly difficult it must have been for the black population in those circumstances. However, we can appreciate how many people still suffer from the aftermath of that era that did not separate people by slavery but made the separation totally on the basis of color. In the Second Reading for today we hear how the Apostle Peter addressed the problem of slavery for Christian slaves in his day. What Peter does is to introduce how God enters the picture of suffering. What he says we can apply to all suffering.

You Are Blessed

Peter begins this section of his letter which is our reading for today with a question. "Now who will harm you if you are eager to do what is good?" Ordinarily, that is true. Under normal circumstances people appreciate when you do the good for them. Yet certainly Peter knew that people crucified Jesus precisely for doing good. We all know that people can turn on us when we think we are being most helpful. The situation Peter was addressing was for the slaves. One can imagine in that circumstance that if a slave volunteered to do good, the master would be accepting. Then again, Peter has to admit, "But even if you do suffer for what is right, you are blessed."

Human nature being what it is, a slave master can be terribly abusive for no reason at all, just like some modern bosses or managers. Yet Peter suggests that under the worst of circumstances any of us would suffer wrongfully, we are blessed. We are blessed, because he says, "Do not fear what they fear, and do not be intimidated, but in your hearts sanctify Christ as Lord." The reason we do not have to be thrown in these unfortunate situations is because our faith in Christ helps us to live beyond our self-concerns. To "sanctify Christ as Lord" is to know that one's immediate concern reaches beyond the one who inflicts the injustice. The one who causes us the suffering or the situation that causes the suffering is not the lord of our lives. The suffering that comes to us is not the end-all of our lives. To know that is to be richly blessed. We learn to deal with our suffering out of the source of God's love and providence for us and with the confidence that we are not alone in the situation. We attack the problem of dealing with our suffering and pain knowing that Jesus Christ is the Lord of our lives.

Defend Your Hope

Peter expands on the thought of not being intimidated by the suffering or the abusers who cause the suffering. He suggests, "Always be ready to make your defense to anyone who demands from you an accounting for the hope that is in you." Any pressures on us, any harassment, provocation, or threats that wear on us call forth from us the kind of mettle of which we are made. Then we can step up to whatever or whoever is troubling us to give an account of ourselves by the hope we have in Christ. William Martin tells of a crucial moment in the career of George Washington in a novel called *Citizen Washington*. The Continental Army was faring poorly in the revolution. The army was under-manned, under-fed, under-clothed, under-armed, and not paid. Defections were all too many. The generals were irate over the pay issue. They called a meeting which was a mutinous act. Washington canceled the meeting, but then called one of his own with the generals. They met at Windsor Tabernacle, a makeshift chapel constructed for the generals' worship. Washington was the last to enter the chapel. He went to the pulpit, drew out huge sheets on which his speech was scrawled out in large letters. It was a brilliant speech about service for the cause of freedom and the necessity of loyalty.

Washington was no great orator. There was considerable rustling until he finished. Then he drew from his pocket a letter from Mr. Jones of the Continental Congress. Washington explained it was a letter on how they could eventually be paid. He tried reading it, fumbled in his pocket for glasses, shamefully put them on, then commented that he not only had grown gray in the service of his country but nearly blind. He read the letter. When he finished, he concluded the generals had read his mind and his heart, bid them good afternoon, and left. The generals unanimously rallied behind him. It was the crowning moment in Washington's career as general. He had given an honest confession of his position and his firm belief in the cause of freedom. He was not intimidated and gave a good defense of his cause. Peter urges Christians to act out of faith in the same way when they are in similar circumstances.

With Gentleness

Peter adds that when we give an account of the hope that is in us we should do it "with gentleness and reverence." That is good counsel. Every one of us can recall situations in which people have behaved very poorly when trying to defend the faith. One does not have to think only of those sophomoric parlor discussions when people loudly debate their religion or what they think they believe. Often that is a part of growing up or taking the faith seriously for the first time. It is a matter of outgrowing Sunday school religion when one had been told what to believe. Peter has in mind those critical moments when faith is on the line.

As campus pastors can tell you, college or university students often find themselves pressed to give an account of the faith. One student reported that he and his buddy were headed for church one Sunday morning. As they left they were greeted at the dormitory door by floormates who were returning from a big night on campus. The night owls asked, "Where are you going?" The faithful answered they were going to church. "To church?" the returnees asked. Then the two young men were able to relate why it was important for them to go to church. Too often Christians feel their defense of the faith requires high-powered and well-phrased theology. What is more important is that they give the simple account of how the faith works for them.

Keep Your Conscience Clear

Peter adds to his instructions the admonition to keep the conscience clear. He writes, "Keep you conscience clear, so that when you are maligned, those who abuse you for our good conduct in Christ may be put to shame." What Peter has in mind here is that if one is maligned for any reason, one should not entertain all the evil notions that can develop in a spirit of rage, anger, hate, and revenge. One should not concentrate on what kind of evil one can spring in retaliation to those who malign us. That would make the conscience sear with guilt. Rather one should concentrate on the example of our Lord Jesus Christ.

One person who heeded Peter's admonition under the worst of circumstances is the Reverend Yung Sen Chen. In the late '40s

Chen, a native of Tawain, was held prisoner by Chinese Nationals in the basement of a Buddhist chapel. They whipped the sides of Chen's hands fifty times, plunged pistols into his ribs, and stuffed a pressure hose into his mouth until he was unconscious. Yet Chen rose to sing "How Great Thou Art" over and over again. The Nationals yelled at him to shut up, but they must have been impressed by him. Chen dreamt that Christ told him he would be set free in nineteen days. In time all of his fellow prisoners were taken out and shot, yet on the nineteenth day he was set free. Those who had abused him were put to shame by his calm and confident example. We cannot predict and we do not know under what circumstances the occasions will present themselves for us to make the same kind of witness. Yet the possibilities are many that can evoke from us a spirit of hate and vengeance to load our consciences with guilt rather than for us to imitate the spirit of Christ's love and grace.

Suffer For Doing Good

Peter thinks beyond the occasions when we may have to suffer under some abuses or harassment by others. There are times when we know we may be of service to others by being willing to suffer. Peter writes, "It is better to suffer for doing good, if suffering should be God's will, than to suffer for doing evil." There are times when we know if we are willing to accept a burden, some pain, or just exert ourselves on behalf of neighbors, we will have to pay a very dear price. Vocational decisions often involve a great deal of pain as people try to determine what is the better or best way for them to decide. Young people face this as they decide on the pursuit of careers. Not all young people carve out for themselves vocational decisions that are based on money or job security. Many are service oriented in careers they know will be demanding and cause them sacrifice.

Think of the many people who have to make vocational changes for reasons that may be forced on them from within the field they serve affected by takeovers, mergers, and the like. Some may occur, however, because there are family related problems. The family may need to move closer to aged or ailing parents who need attention. No doubt, we could take inventory of any given congregation on a Sunday morning and find numerous families struggling with questions about how they can best serve family needs involving suffering and sacrifice. These are the situations that Peter is referring to when he writes, "It is better to suffer for doing good, if suffering should be God's will." It is not difficult to size up the situations demanding suffering for good. What we can do is to measure them against God's will, and work to discover how we can best serve God's will in taking on that kind of suffering. Peter moves on to show how we not only have the best model for making those decisions but also the best resource for finding the strength to do so. Peter refers to our Lord Jesus Christ to make the point.

The Living Proof

Peter's effort to encourage us to see some blessing in suffering for the sake of good was not manipulation or playing games with words. Peter offers the hard evidence that suffering for doing good is not only exemplified by the Lord Jesus Christ, but also gives assurance of the wholesome outcome of such suffering. He writes, "For Christ also suffered for sins once for all, the righteous for the unrighteous, in order to bring you to God." He goes on that Christ was put to death bodily, but God made him alive in the spirit. The Risen Lord Jesus Christ "went and made a proclamation to the spirits in prison." This is a difficult passage, but we take it to mean that the Risen Christ went and proclaimed his victory over death and the devil to those who had been disobedient and had not believed. Peter indicates that this is not the way God wanted it.

Peter relates how God had been extremely patient during the time of the building of Noah's ark. The time of 120 years for the building of the ark was a time of grace. Witnesses to the ark could have been invited on board the ark. Instead, they were lost in the drowning waters. Not so for Noah. He and his family were saved. The passenger list consisted of only eight people who were the faithful who believed the word of God. Peter says the flood was their baptism. The waters that destroyed others became the waters of salvation for the Noachian family. Peter uses the story of the flood to illustrate the fact that God is constantly reversing what

126

people normally expect. Noah's boat building cost him a price and some suffering while his neighbors laughed. Like the people who laughed at Fulton's folly, the first steam boat, the crowd heehawed at Noah's folly until the ark was raised off the land in a baptism of grace for Noah and company.

How God Works

The salvation of Noah and his family in this remarkable baptism, Peter continues, prefigured our baptism into the Lord Jesus Christ. Our baptism into the Lord Jesus was not simply a ritual cleansing but "an appeal to God for a clean conscience." What Peter indicates is that through the death of our Lord Jesus Christ, God was able to raise Jesus from the dead to make it very plain that through suffering and death God raises us to a new life. The suffering, death, and resurrection of our Lord Jesus Christ demonstrate how God operates. In 1518 Martin Luther wrote the *Heidelberg Disputation*, a defense of the theology he had launched with the writing of his 95 Theses. In one of the theses of the Heidelberg work, Luther wrote that most people do not know God hidden in suffering. Normally they hate the cross and suffering. They are apt to call the cross evil, and what they call good are the flawed works of people.

However, it is by faith that we recognize God in suffering and at the cross. Peter says through that faith we are able to share in the victory of our Lord through his suffering and death by which he has gone to heaven and is at the right hand of God ruling over all authorities and powers. The artist Salvador Dali helps us understand Peter's explanation of the cross. Dali painted the cross suspended high above the earth. The painting was designed to reflect the words of our Lord, "And I, when I am lifted up from the earth, will draw all people to myself" (John 12:32). Through the cross and its suffering Christ draws us to himself. The painting is the artist's means of expressing how Christ welcomed suffering and the cross to achieve salvation for us. Peter encourages us to understand the cross as means of transforming suffering for the sake of the good. Luther would say that thus a theology of the cross enables us to see things as they really are, enables us to call things as they really are, and, above all, to see the blessing in suffering. Luther would warn us against building our own crosses. Enough will come on their own, but when they do, God will help us to make them a blessing.

Ascension Of The Lord
Ephesians 1:15-23

Having High Hope

Into Thin Air is John Krakauer's grizzly account of the loss of twelve persons attempting to climb Mount Everest. Krakauer himself was a member of one of the parties making the effort to reach the peak of Everest. His account reads like a novel and it is hard to put down. The most fascinating feature of this story is trying to decipher what drives people to attempt the adventure of climbing the highest peak in the world. People pay exorbitant amounts of money to be led by veteran guides and teams of leaders who have led many people up the mount. Many have succeeded with good guidance. Some have not reached the top. Some died on the way.

The trails up the mount are littered with the remains of sporting people who have failed. To be sure, there are those sports figures who love the dare involved. There are adventuresome people who like any kind of challenge. There are those who climb only because the mountain is there. An underlying feature for all is a common urge. The majestic heights of the mountain beckon all who see it to explore its beauty and wonder. Krakauer heads each of his chapters recounting this mystic venture with quotes from other people who have made the effort to climb Everest. One climber surmised that he had been lured into an ephemeral climb in search of something he had already left behind. That observation is a parabolic warning that on this Ascension Day we could be looking for something beyond us and lose sight of what our Lord has gained for us by his ascension into thin air.

Enlightenment

The event of the Ascension of our Lord is recorded in the First Reading and the Holy Gospel appointed for this day. The story is well known. What is important to note is that it is Luke who informs us that over a period of forty days Jesus appeared to the disciples. Jesus used the time to assure the disciples of his resurrection and that they would eventually understand the significance of what he had taught them in the light of his death and resurrection. Through the process of recalling and researching what Jesus had taught them and done for them, they would discover that the acts of Jesus would be entirely consistent with what God had revealed through the history of Israel. Through that process of searching his life, death, and resurrection and matching his work with what God had previously revealed to their people, they came to understand more fully by the power of the Holy Spirit whom God would send them. They would be enlightened by the Spirit.

In the Second Reading for Ascension we hear the apostolic description of what our Lord Jesus Christ continues to do for us. We assume it is Paul who is writing. He says, "I pray that the God of our Lord Jesus Christ, the Father of glory, may give you the spirit of wisdom and revelation as you come to know him so that with the eyes of your heart enlightened, you may know him." That is why our Lord ascended to the Father. Jesus ascended that we might come to know the Father better. What the Father reveals to us is that God would have us to know our relationship with God through our Lord Jesus Christ. What we learn thereby is not some set of formulas, rules, or facts that we must do to be on better terms with God. Rather we learn that God has already indicated how God was willing to enter life on the same terms as we to make sure we can understand God's love for us.

Hope

Essentially, what God has done for us in Jesus of Nazareth is to call us to share life with the Christ. Paul writes, "So that you may know what is the hope to which he has called you." As Paul employs the word "hope" here, we should recognize that Paul writes of "hope" as a unique Christian experience. For Paul, hope in Christ is the absolute assurance that what God has done for us and what God promises to do in the future is divine reality. This understanding of hope is not that something might happen to provide a happy ending, a good solution, or a bonanza of some sort. Hope in the Hebrew Scriptures is always expressed in terms of the mighty acts of God. God is the hope of Israel because of what God has done and will continue to do for God's people.

In the New Testament it is the resurrection of our Lord Jesus Christ that is the mighty act of God. Consequently, our Risen Lord Jesus Christ is our hope. Our hope rests solidly on all that culminates in and is affirmed by the resurrection of our Lord. That implies all that was revealed in the life, death, and resurrection of Jesus of Nazareth builds up into this sure and certain hope. Paul's understanding of this hope in Christ Jesus has absolutely no relationship to worldly or human achievement. Utopian and secular optimism are totally alien to this revelation of hope in Christ. The origin of this hope is in the resurrection of Jesus, and its promise of the future is in the return of our Lord Jesus Christ. For that reason on the day of the Ascension of our Lord that hope is revitalized and renewed as we rehearse the Ascension event as a sign of promise that our Lord will return. That hope gives new meaning to our lives, refreshes our spirits, and gives us the certainty that our work is not in vain.

The Glorious Inheritance

With the hope we share in our Lord Jesus Christ comes the inheritance we will also share with him. When we celebrate the Ascension of our Lord, we recall how Jesus returned to the Father to enjoy what the Father had been holding for him. What our Lord could claim as the Son of the Father was the right to God's kingly rule. Paul writes about "the riches of his glorious inheritance among the saints." The very reason that Jesus entered into the human condition was to enable people to enjoy the same benefactions he received. Elsewhere Paul can write about the believers in our Lord Jesus Christ as those who have been adopted by God. In ancient times adoption was created as a procedure to enable the childless wealthy man or woman to pass on an estate to an heir. By grace we have been adopted into the family of God to be God's true heirs with the Lord Jesus Christ.

As sons and daughters of God we are privileged to share with the Son of God. We are afforded the right to share in the kingly rule, eternal life, and a life of righteousness. We have not experienced the ultimate of what that means. What we do have now as the heirs with the Lord Jesus is the assurance that sharing his kingdom will happen. While Jesus was on the earth, while he suffered death and entered into the resurrection, Jesus was always the heir, even though he was in this life. The same holds true for us. We are the heirs of the kingdom with the Lord Jesus. That is certain. It is sure and certain as our hope. However, there is the "not yet" feature of our inheritance. While we are in this world, with whatever conditions, handicaps, trials, or tribulations we have, we are heirs of the kingdom. Or if our lives are serene and calm, devoid of trial and hardship, we also sense the "not yet" of faith.

Immeasurable Greatness

If our talk about our inheritance as the adopted children of God appears to be only about our future, Paul corrects that notion. Along with the expressions concerning our hope and inheritance as the children of God, Paul maintains we are in position to understand "what is the immeasurable greatness of his power ... according to the working of his great power." This means we can examine the creation with a new understanding of what God is doing within the creation not simply as happenstance and accidental products of Mother Nature, but we see our providential Heavenly Father providing for us, God's creatures. We witness the storming and erratic behavior of natural forces within the creation not simply as accidental freaks of nature, but we see the hand of God writing warnings in big letters of greater judgments to come. Ordinarily people balk at any interpretation of natural catastrophes as judgments of God. To be sure, we cannot assume, as our Lord Jesus Christ himself said, that the victims of natural disasters have sinned more and are more deserving of judgment. The disruptions of the creation rather are calls for us all to repent.

Paul writes that those who believe can take note how God uses the immeasurable greatness of divine power to give everyone a wake up call to God's presence within the creation. If people fail to see the goodness and grace of God at work within the vastness and finiteness of the creation, then God has to shake them up by a negative expression of divine power. Airiness, one of the early church fathers, believed there were four Gospels, because there were four zones within the creation and four great winds within the creation. Today we would hardly subscribe to such a simplistic notion. Yet for his moment, the church father saw the gospel related to God's power within the universes. For our day, we have every reason to believe the same as our understanding of the universes expands.

The Power At Work

However, Paul would have us realize that God employs divine power in more than the creation. Paul writes, "God put this power to work in Christ when he raised him from the dead and seated him at his right hand in heavenly places." The full potential of God's power is not known by what God can and does do in the universe. That use of power of itself is awesome. However, in the death and resurrection of our Lord Jesus Christ, God demonstrated the divine power over life and death. That is how God gave the evidence of the best and most of what God can do for us. When God gives life in the form of the tiny infant, we see the divine power at work in creating a remarkable gift who will grow with its wisps of hair, tiny fingernails, and little shining eyes. Yet when that body grows to old age deformed by calcification of arthritis, dimmed in the eyes, and wrinkled with pain, we can surrender it to the grave. Yet we not only surrender it to the maggots of decay but to the sure and certain hope of the resurrection from the dead.

Niteline once featured a story of a medical experiment on Mount Everest, the same mountain mentioned in the introduction. The experiment was to research the behavior of the heart under the trying circumstances of thin air. The air is so thin on the mountain that the oxygen is about one third of what we naturally breathe. The purpose of the study would be to determine what we can learn about the heart in trying circumstances. So the ascent of Mount Everest would have the benefit of helping us to live longer. What we learn from Paul is that the ascent of our Risen Lord to heavenly places is to afford us the benefit that God will raise us from the dead for eternity.

Above All Authority

God's use of authority through our Lord Jesus Christ goes much deeper than God's promise and ability to raise us from the dead. When God raised God's Son from the dead and admitted him into God's kingdom and under God's kingly rule, Paul writes, God "put all things under his feet." He further explains this to mean that we are to take this literally.

Our Lord Jesus Christ rules "far above all rule and authority and power and dominion, and above every name that is named, not only in this age but also in the age to come." The practical application of the rule of Christ is that whether there is a Republican or a Democrat in the White House, Christ is ruler over all. Whether any nation rises to upset the international hold on the use of nuclear power, Christ is still ruler over all. That is true about all earthly power or wherever we locate power.

Whether we are talking about the powers that be in the governor's office, city hall, the university, the business conglomerate, or within the home, Christ is ruler over all. We tend to lose sight of that. One can understand why. We live under power; we work under power. We may be in position to employ power ourselves. It is reality to say that if we want to get something done, we have to get to the powers that be. However, we can be sure that the abuses of power, the false uses of power, and the misuse of power will ultimately fail, because Christ rules over all. The *History Channel* has aired the fall of Napoleon, one of the most outstanding figures in all of history. The same program has chronicled the fall of the Third Reich and the end of the Holocaust. Other programs have included the collapse of segregation in our own country, the fall of the Berlin Wall in Germany, and the collapse of the USSR. Christ does rule over every power and dominion.

134

The Head Of The Church

Having recognized our Lord's complete and full use of power over all other powers in the world, Paul concludes with the statement that God has made Our Lord Jesus Christ "the head over all things for the church, which is his body, the fullness of him who fills all in all." The striking feature of this observation is that Paul indicates that Christ uses the powers of divine majesty to rule all things for the sake of the church. One would never guess that possibility when one reads secular assessments of the role of the church in the world. For some writers it is popular to make the church fair game in writing of the diminishing role or power of the church in the world. Paul would never agree to that. Paul would insist that it is only because of the existence of and the presence of the church in the world, that the world still stands. It is only by faith we recognize this to be true.

By faith we know the realities of the history being made around us, and Paul would say, for us. For example, our nation was totally absorbed by the production of the movie *Titanic*. The film got a number of academy awards and still stimulates considerable interest years afterward. Yet the film trivialized the event by centering on it as an occasion for a love story. The lesson to be learned from that shocking event was what William Lord called *A Night to Remember* in his excellent account of the tragedy that it was. Lord saw the sinking of that marvelous ship as an incident that shook the confidence of a world in a year in which people optimistically believed it could create an unsinkable ship like it could rule and do anything it wanted to do. Faith recognizes otherwise. Just as we, the people of God, know God rules all things in our interest and welfare. We can read the negative signs of the rule and judgment of Christ in the world. We also recognize the manner in which he also serves humanity through the great heroes of faith. For us this means the certainty of the Presence of the Christ in our lives. Jesus, our Lord and Christ, did not ascend into the thin air to vanish, but he broke a trail for us that he might be present with us at all times and lead us into eternity.

Surprised By Suffering?

Belva Plain wrote about a battered housewife back when our national conscience was awaking to the serious problem of domestic violence. Plain's novel *Whispers* takes place in the comfortable affluent home of Robert Ferguson, a rising star in the corporate world. He and his wife Lynn are the parents of two daughters, Ann and Emily, and a son, Robert. An infant daughter had been lost in a swimming pool drowning.

The father is bright, handsome, winsome, thoughtful, and apparently very loving. On occasion, however, he is extremely physically violent with his wife Lynn. With his daughters he is harsh and cruel emotionally. It is obvious he can neither be contradicted nor challenged in making any major decision for his family. Each time Robert becomes violent with Lynn, he becomes exceedingly remorseful, but he always finds an excuse for his dreadful tantrums.

The periods between the horrible incidents are filled with warmth and devotion for Lynn and his family. Over and over again Lynn is completely surprised at how Robert can be so mean. She is equally surprised that she still loves him and does not want to believe him capable of more terror. Lynn's dilemma is a common one. Her confused state is common to the battered wives and children of our society who continue to be surprised by the evil their loved one is able to force on them. However, the whole society continues to be shocked by any form of suffering, evil, pain, or hardship individuals force on our homes, community, and society as a whole. Much of our evening news introduces new surprises, shocks, and puzzles of how perverse humanity can be. In the Second Reading appointed for today we hear the Apostle Peter say to us that we should not be shocked by any kind of suffering that comes along.

The Fiery Ordeal

The kind of suffering Peter had in mind was the persecutions which Christians were beginning to experience because of their faith. Fortunately, we in America do not have to contend with that problem for the moment. Yet there are those who predict that it will not always be so in America. The churches have lost favor in some communities. Also the development of severe shortages of clergy may make churches more vulnerable to attack in the future. Presently, however, there are good Christian people in other parts of the world who suffer the fiery ordeal because of the faith. We recognize that century-old tensions between Muslims and Christians in the Balkan states have not really subsided.

We are embarrassed by the long-standing feud between Irish Catholics and Protestants. The Middle East tensions between Christians and Jews are hidden in the open conflicts of national politics. The plight of many Christians suffering persecutions in Africa is part of the ongoing news flowing from that continent. We should not be surprised if the growing populations of Eastern religions within our own American borders do not create the kind of tensions that are difficult for some Christians to bear as the Christian faith continues to lose favor in the society. The point is that American Christians must get used to the idea that the faith can never live within this world without the threat of the fiery trial of persecution always lurking as a possibility. Peter would just want you to know that the gospel has many enemies. Persecution is always a threat.

Fiery Ordeals

However, we should not think of persecution as the only severe testing of the faith. Peter wrote, "Beloved, do not be surprised at the fiery ordeal that is taking place among you to test you, as though something strange were happening to you." We have to think of any testing of the faith as equally dangerous. In our society we do not have to think of the government as spoiling or destroying the faith of our youth. During the Hitler regime in Nazi Germany, the government did not forcibly take the children away from their churches. The government simply ran youth programs on Sundays mornings to compete with the churches. How different is that from our own communities that run program after program for the youth on Sunday mornings? The thought is never expressed that the youth programs are designed to take our children away from their churches. The leaders just do not think of the churches.

One has to recall how, under the worst conditions for the Christian churches in the Roman Empire, Christian believers lost their lives when they refused to offer a sacrifice to the Roman emperor or gods. How easy it would have been for the Christians to excuse themselves for making a little gesture to satisfy their persecutors. If one gives the problem some thought, one has to come to the conclusion that our loss to the youth programs which interfere with the faith of our children is equally blatant or more so than the sprinkling of incense on the altar of an alien god. Someone is going to say it is not fair to pick on the youth programs. To be sure, there are oodles of competing forces that create tests of faith for us. However, the Sunday morning youth programs are obvious competition and highly tempting for the faith. Who wants to jeopardize the child's starting position in the lineup by going to church instead of the practice or a game?

More Trials

The fiery trials and testing of the faith also come in other disguises and wear other masks, such as illness in the family, economic problems, and vocational distress. Everyone in this congregation this morning could name a private testing that he/she has gone through. John Gould, a teacher at Phillips Academy in Andover, Massachusetts, gives us an account of an ordeal that fell to his family. His story is *The Withering Child*, an account of how his five-year-old son became anorectic during John's welcome study sabbatical in England. The son, Gardner, became immobilized over a ten-week period, and Gould had to give up his study plans that would have been most helpful in his career as a teacher. The record Gould shares is a nightmarish account of the struggle to deal with this darling boy who was literally wasting away. Gardner retches and fidgets as the parents seek to find what is troubling their son.

What is especially difficult to handle is the guilt the parents feel in why this may have happened to their son, and how they have to find release from that guilt to be able to love again. That is an enormous testing of the faith that comes to parents, families, and friends of people who find illness and handicaps as their special trials. Peter's observation that we should not be shocked when trials come, in whatever form they do, should free us to take heart in the fact that we are sharing in Christ's sufferings. No matter how the testing runs over, through, or into our lives, we know our Lord Jesus Christ had to suffer through the same. We know God strengthened him to do so, and he gained the victory. So, says Peter, "You may also be glad and shout for joy when his glory is revealed." Peter's point is, even though we have to share in our Lord's suffering with our own form of suffering, we are also going to be there for the shouting to share in the glory when our Lord Jesus Christ shows up in glory.

Humble Yourself

Our reading moves ahead towards the close of Peter's letter to pick up some good advice for dealing with what we have to suffer and endure. The first piece of this counsel is, "Humble yourselves therefore under the mighty hand of God, so that he may exalt you in due time." Peter most certainly was not suggesting we grovel before God and beat ourselves down. Here Peter is not talking about the kind of humility we must assume as we confess our sins and pray for God's forgiveness. Rather the emphasis here is on the humility necessary for us to recognize how helpless we are apart from the "mighty hand of God." We are to own up to our weakened state. We do need help. We are not God. God waits for us to call upon God for divine help. Peter says, "Cast all your anxiety on him, because he cares for you."

All good parents are eager to help their children in their times of need. Quite often parents are chagrined that their children did not call for help and got themselves into very deep trouble. Sometimes the call from the children comes too late. God urges us to call. God stands over us as a father or mother and waits. The Prophet Isaiah assures us we can call. "You shall cry for help, and he will say, Here I am" (Isaiah 58:9). We all know people who make life too difficult for themselves because they do not know how to ask for help. They may feel asking for help is a weakness of character. This often happens to senior citizens who keep saying, "I do not want to become a bother or a burden for someone." Probably none of us want to let that happen to us in our time of need. Yet when we need help as the aged, the sick, or the immobilized individuals, we do our friends and family a better service by letting them help and cooperating with them. In our relationship with God, Luther would say, "Let God be God." Let God have God's way with us by helping us. God could not be more pleased.

Discipline Yourself

You can be sure God is not going to do too much for us. God is not going to spoil us. If, on the one hand, God does not permit us to have to handle more than we can bear, it is also true God does not want to make our dependency upon God obsolete. That is why Peter can write, "Cast all your anxiety on him, because he cares for you." With the next scratch of the pen, he writes, "Discipline yourselves, keep alert." We introduced Peter's attitude toward suffering with the abusive treatment Lynn Ferguson suffered at the hands of her husband Robert in the novel *Whispers*. In one of his monthly columns (*The Lutheran*, May, 2000), Walter Wangerin, Jr., wrote about how he handled his adopted African-American daughter Talitha. Talitha had experienced trauma in the shock of adoption, leaving her familiar surroundings at the age of eight months. He referred to the trauma he himself had suffered as a child. Wangerin related how for both himself and his daughter there had to be a lot of confession and much prayer for help. However, there also had to be a good deal of help from his wife, Thanne, as well as the presence and help from God.

What is important to understand about the Wangerins is that neither father nor daughter had to resign themselves as victims for whom the pain was so deep there can be no help. With the spiritual disciplines of prayer, grace, and forgiveness, help is available to achieve a wholesome attitude towards oneself and others. Staying fit in the wake of disastrous experiences is also preparation for whatever else is to come in the future. Peter would impress upon us that there is always more to come. "Keep alert," he writes, like "a roaring lion your adversary the devil prowls around looking for someone to devour." One does not have to look far to realize how the demonic shows up in all kind of shapes, forms, and disguises. The roaring lion is also accompanied by wolves who come to us in sheep's clothing (Matthew 7:15). No matter what mask the demons wear, we can be sure that in one form or another, the basic temptation is somehow the same. In one way or another the tempting suggestion will be you cannot trust in a gracious God. We can recognize that suggestion behind its disguise and sniff out the presence of the lion who is stalking us.

In The Same Boat

Peter would not want his readers to think that he was singling them out as unique people who had to deal with suffering, or that suffering would be only in their culture or their era. Rather Peter urges the faithful to resist the devil, "Steadfast in your faith, for you know that your brothers and sisters in all the world are undergoing the same kinds of suffering." Temptations or suffering are common to all people. Peter may have had in mind how Christians all around the Roman Empire were suffering persecution, but we can be sure his words are appropriate for all people suffering temptation everywhere at any time. Peter suffered temptation right under the very nose of Jesus in the courtyard of the high priest. Peter could talk from experience.

Two years before his death, in 1962, General Douglas MacArthur addressed the student body of cadets at West Point. As a literary piece the speech has to rank among the finest of public addresses on record. In part, MacArthur said, "From your ranks come the great captains who hold the nation's destiny in their hands the moment the war tocsin sounds ... This does not mean that you are warmongers. On the contrary, the soldier, above all other people, prays for peace, for he must suffer and bear the deepest wounds and scars of war. But always in our ears ring the ominous words of Plato, that wisest of all philosophers: 'Only the dead have seen the end of war' " (quoted in *Parade* magazine, May 7, 2000). Tacking the General's comments on to the Apostle Peter, no one can escape the suffering and pain of war and death that plague our world. Peter's encouragement for us is to keep aware of how things really are and resist the evil as it comes to us.

The Final Word

The bottom line Peter draws under all his talk about suffering is, "And after you have suffered for a little while, the God of all grace, who has called you to his eternal glory in Christ, will himself restore, support, strengthen, and establish you." What Peter says is far more profound than the little comfort people offer when they say, "This, too will pass." People can dig in the barrel for all kinds of sayings like that. "Suffering is better than the alternative." Or they can find comfort in the greater trials and sufferings they see someone else enduring, "I thought I had it bad until I saw what Joe has to bear." Or that easy one, "It's not the end of the world," or "Things could be worse." You can add the bromides you have heard. If you want to hear stuff like these stabs at bringing comfort, sit in the lobby of the doctor's office for an hour or so. You could also go to the surgery waiting room at the hospital. This kind of talk can be cruel if people are not able to understand or know the real reason why there is the suffering, how one can cope with the suffering, and what the ultimate outcome of the suffering will be.

Becker is a television situation comedy about John Becker, a medical doctor. In one episode the doctor gets into a hassle with a priest about treating a patient. The priest warms to Becker when he realizes how personally concerned Becker is about the welfare of his patient, who turns out to be the priest's brother. Becker becomes more uneasy about his attitude toward the priest because of Becker's personal feelings about the faith. Becker confesses to be an atheist. However, he is touched by the persistence of the priest who obviously has much to offer his brother because of the faith. That is what Peter offers us. The word Peter shares with us does not come from the bottom of the barrel of easy quips in the waiting room. What is offered is from the heart of God of all grace who made sure we could be strengthened, restored, and renewed in the face of all temptation and suffering through the glory of our Lord Jesus Christ. Peter tags on a final word to all of that, "To him be the power forever and ever. Amen." Oh, yes, and one more, "Peace to all of you who are in Christ."

Books In This Cycle A Series

GOSPEL SET
It's News To Me! Messages Of Hope For Those Who Haven't Heard
Sermons For Advent/Christmas/Epiphany
Linda Schiphorst McCoy

Tears Of Sadness, Tears Of Gladness
Sermons For Lent/Easter
Albert G. Butzer, III

Pentecost Fire: Preaching Community In Seasons Of Change
Sermons For Sundays After Pentecost (First Third)
Schuyler Rhodes

Questions Of Faith
Sermons For Sundays After Pentecost (Middle Third)
Marilyn Saure Breckenridge

The Home Stretch: Matthew's Vision Of Servanthood In The End-Time
Sermons For Sundays After Pentecost (Last Third)
Mary Sue Dehmlow Dreier

FIRST LESSON SET
Long Time Coming!
Sermons For Advent/Christmas/Epiphany
Stephen M. Crotts

Restoring The Future
Sermons For Lent/Easter
Robert J. Elder

Formed By A Dream
Sermons For Sundays After Pentecost (First Third)
Kristin Borsgard Wee

Living On One Day's Rations
Sermons For Sundays After Pentecost (Middle Third)
Douglas B. Bailey

Let's Get Committed
Sermons For Sundays After Pentecost (Last Third)
Derl G. Keefer

SECOND LESSON SET

Holy E-Mail
Sermons For Advent/Christmas/Epiphany
Dallas A. Brauninger

Access To High Hope
Sermons For Lent/Easter
Harry N. Huxhold

Acting On The Absurd
Sermons For Sundays After Pentecost (First Third)
Gary L. Carver

A Call To Love
Sermons For Sundays After Pentecost (Middle Third)
Tom M. Garrison

Distinctively Different
Sermons For Sundays After Pentecost (Last Third)
Gary L. Carver